T0146829

THROUGH A PILOT'S WINDOW

Adventures Piloting a B-24 Bomber in the 9th and 344th Bomber Squadron in WWII During the Asian-Pacific, European and African Middle Eastern Campaigns, 1942-1945

A MEMOIR
by
Lt. Col. William McKean Gilbert

Foreword by
Kate Gilbert Friedman

THROUGH A PILOT'S WINDOW
Adventures Piloting a B-24 Bomber in the 9th and 344th Bomber Squadron in WWII During the Asian-Pacific, European and African Middle Eastern Campaigns, 1942-1945

Copyright © 2016 Kate Gilbert Friedman.

All rights reserved. No part of this book may be used or reproduced by any means, graphic, electronic, or mechanical, including photocopying, recording, taping or by any information storage retrieval system without the written permission of the author except in the case of brief quotations embodied in critical articles and reviews.

iUniverse books may be ordered through booksellers or by contacting:

iUniverse
1663 Liberty Drive
Bloomington, IN 47403
www.iuniverse.com
1-800-Authors (1-800-288-4677)

Because of the dynamic nature of the Internet, any web addresses or links contained in this book may have changed since publication and may no longer be valid. The views expressed in this work are solely those of the author and do not necessarily reflect the views of the publisher, and the publisher hereby disclaims any responsibility for them.

Any people depicted in stock imagery provided by Thinkstock are models, and such images are being used for illustrative purposes only. Certain stock imagery © Thinkstock.

ISBN: 978-1-5320-0126-0 (sc)
ISBN: 978-1-5320-0127-7 (hc)
ISBN: 978-1-5320-0128-4 (e)

Library of Congress Control Number: 2016913616

Print information available on the last page.

iUniverse rev. date: 11/29/2016

TABLE OF CONTENTS

The pilot's window is in his plane and his mind. Through it he sees the world huddled together as his parents never imagined. But he, too, like the Americans who said: "It can't happen to us," comes to know that his fragile wall of glass can only deflect air. From bullets and shocking realities it will not shield.

This book is dedicated to the men herein who died in the hope of achieving peace. Only we who live will suffer if America fails to safeguard that peace unselfishly.

The names, but not the actions or thoughts, of the characters are fictional. A few persons mentioned in passing retain their real names.

Lt. Col. Wm. Gilbert

ILLUSTRATIONS

FOREWORD

I had no idea where my father grew up until the year my husband and I moved two thousand miles from our home in California to Illinois and bought a house on Park Place. Just like in Monopoly.

I called mom to give her my new address in Evanston, IL.

"Oh," she hesitated, "I think that's the street your dad grew up on?"

"No way." The coincidence was hard to believe.

We'd bought our house so fast, I wanted to see how well we'd done and we went to the Open House across the street. When I turned to the realtor I couldn't believe the lady's nose: it was my dad's nose. Now my father's nose was unmistakable, and I was stunned. I walked up to her and asked, "Does the name Bill Gilbert mean anything to you?"

"Yes," she stared at me, "Bill is my cousin. I bought his parents' home down the street."

I felt faint. It can't be true: a fantastic coincidence.

But in fact my dad did grow up on Park Place, in Evanston, Illinois.

He played football for DePauw University in Indiana, and when he graduated in 1940, he joined the Air Force. By joining up he may partly have wanted to honor a family tradition that runs back three hundred years from 1634 when our earliest American ancestor, Coronet Robert Stetson, protected the Pilgrims, to my great-great-grandfather Senator David Jewett Baker, Lincoln's key political ally in Illinois, and to the Lincoln–Douglas debates held on Senator Baker's lawn in Alton, Illinois, and to my grandmother, Esther Miller, the first woman student at Northwestern University. Esther married Wm. C. Gilbert. Together they raised my dad, Bill, in the old family home on Park Place.

My father's memoirs as a pilot would fascinate my son, I realized, the year he turned ten and I needed something exciting for him to read. I managed to get ahold of the typed manuscript he had left in a box. The box was filled with delicate pages of blue ink typed on onion-skin paper, so thin and fragile, the old typewriter's metal letters had made holes through all the letter o's. Many of its pages were stuck together by now, whole paragraphs nearly indecipherable, words so smudged they had to be decoded, and the entire manuscript edited, retyped, edited, retyped, and so on—but the resulting book was worth every hour spent on it.

My father was one of the surviving members of the elite 9th bombing squadron, who were assigned to fly missions over the Middle East. The B-24 bombers they flew close to the ground were dangerously effective, but also fat targets for the enemy. Many of my father's buddies went down amid ack-ack bursts from below and the hellfire of Japanese Zeroes. Time and again though, my dad's plane made it through.

This book, however, isn't only about guts and warfare. What makes it particularly interesting are my father's observations when he's on the ground on leave, his take on the variety of people he lives among and the unfamiliar countries he lives in during a slice of time when Israel, then known as Palestine, was occupied by the British. To my dad, a kid from the Midwest, everything abroad seemed so strange, so new.

His descriptions here are always pointedly sharp and he leaves very little out. He writes about everything, about guides and dancers, brawls and shrines, gambling and friendship, even about the half-Arab woman he lived with and most likely loved.

As I read his memoirs I could see my father, an easy-going, friendly lad in his early 20s barely out of college, now trained to fly an enormous bomber, a tackle on the Depauw University football team, now looking out through a small window set back from the bomber's nose, at the deadly war in Southeast Asia and the lively world of the Mideast.

Kate Gilbert Friedman

Chapter I

TRANSITION

I sat back and laughed with enjoyment as the sweat streamed down the pimples of Tanner's red face. He gunned first #4 motor. Then all four engines together, trying to rock the giant left wheel of our B-24 out of a sand hole. His forehead and chin, both slanting back from the tip of his small pointed nose, made him look like a fox at bay. He had always treated his big bomber like a pursuit ship -- a "pea-shooter" -- but now he was feeling its 50,000 pounds. All my hours as a terror-stricken co-pilot were beyond the bump on the lovely homeward slope. But Tanner had gotten stuck. On top of that, he had come within a fraction of twisting the left landing gear off. The final deep-throated gasp and blurp of the engines signaled his admission of defeat. Two master sergeants and a major had just reached the plane from the engineering area.

"Who in hell is the pilot of this thing?"

"The wingtip's nearly on the ground."

"That gear's ready to come off. Keep everybody from under the wing!"

We opened the bomb bay doors, and I was careful to let Tanner crawl out first. All Tanner's hours of sweating out steep turns had resulted in one long wing pointed straight up; the other straight down only 500 feet above ground, was about to make another record. But I was about to forgive those pursuit landings, because I was going to get a new pilot. That was being settled by the conversations outside.

Instead of taxiing on the paved strips that formed a small triangle, Tanner had tried to gun the ship across the triangle through soft sand, and the great left tire had uncovered a hole. (Tanner had accomplished the rest). It took days of jacking and minor repairing before the ship was safe to fly from our Florida field to the repair depot at Tampa. By that time I had a new pilot.

Ed Thompson had been on leave the first two weeks I was in the squadron. Major (then Captain) Sturgis told me Thompson would be my pilot, so the first time I saw him shuffling down on the path by our pup tents, I anxiously tried to know him on first sight. We were to go into combat together within a month. He was fairly thin and his shoulders tended to stoop just a little. He was my height -- about 5'11", dark hair and complexion. His cheeks were a bit sunken, and there were lines in his face that suggested calloused-hand knowledge of hard work. When he looked at me, his dark eyes were honestly noncommittal, but there was pleasantness in the lines of his mouth.

"Thompson?" I said. "I guess I'm your new co-pilot."

"Guess so," he answered unemotionally, and stuck out his hand. He didn't smile. I had no way of knowing then that he was frightened at being a first pilot with only 30 hours in a B-24.

That was just about the extent or our acquaintance until our own ship arrived. The first pilots did most of the flying and training the next three weeks. Ed and I flew together about twice before the bombardier, Gimble, and navigator, Swetland, joined the crew. Gimble had been in another squadron of the same group before being transferred to ours.

I knew him by his animated friendliness and admirable physique before I knew we were assigned together. He was blond with a rosy complexion, and was about 6' 2". Usually happy and carefree as a puppy, he thought ill of almost no one but himself – and that at long-separated intervals.

At practically the last minute, four navigators (they were straight from school) arrived in the operations tent. Someone tossed a coin and Swetland came with us, while his close friend, Bradson, was put on the Squadron C.O.'s crew. Our crew was Capt. Rodger Sturgis, now a full Colonel and holder of the Congressional Medal of Honor. His is almost as legendary name now, but he was just as hardworking, much-loved Captain when I joined his squadron. His men a year later had grown to like him less.

Paul Swetland was a nice guy. In a sweet way, he was a "mother's boy," yet men admired him because he was interested in a great many things, was talented, and showed good taste in whatever he did. He was an only child whose father had died while he was in navigation school. I remember seeing his luxurious Buick standing across the sandy road from our tent area, and his mother was sitting at the wheel waiting. Paul felt he should eat with us at the officers' mess tent that first day, so Mrs. Swetland patiently waited until Paul was sure he had no duties for the afternoon, and was free to go into town where she had a room. I have never before or since known a mother and son who were as close as those two were. There was a mutual feeling of complete responsibility and intimacy.

The four officers of the crew became acquainted first on a trip we made to Albuquerque for some practice bombing. We didn't see much of Swetland, because the work was chiefly with the bombardiers and pilots. I got to know Jerry's – Gimble's – voice over the interphone as he talked us on course, described where the bombs hit, or swore through the explanation of an error. At Ed's suggestion, Jerry showed the two of us how to operate the synthetic bomb trainer so that we would know more about the working of the bombsight and understand some of the bombardier's troubles.

Ed and I stayed at the field, but Jerry had a room in a hotel with Swetland and two Air Corps wolves who were with us. About nine o'clock one night, Paul, stripped to a pair of shorts, was quietly reading a book in the room, when one of the boys strolled in with a nice-looking girl. In an embarrassed frenzy, Paul stumbled into pants and shirt, begging pardon all the way.

When I saw him the next day, he looked tired, and I told him so.

"Shucks," he said, grinning like a school kid, "The guy wasn't in the room more than ten minutes when he practically shoved me out the door and said he was sorry. I wanted to go to a movie. Heck! I didn't want coffee. Then I called the room until the hotel operator sounded sore, but nobody answered. I finally came out here about midnight and got a room."

The three of us, without Swetland, would show up at the Casanova in town for a beer and to check the prospects for a date among the girls gathered there. At the jute box began a ribbing that Jerry continued around the world. His favorite recording was Nelson Eddy's rendition of "Ride, Cossack, Ride." He played it about fifteen times a night for the four days we were there, until Thompson and I just about carried out our threat of mayhem if he ever played it again. We heard that recording in the Near East, the Middle East, and the Far East until we screamed, grew numb to it. Then decided it might have some merit, and finally played it ourselves. War does terrible things to a man's musical sense.

For weeks, we had been wondering where we would go. I started wondering when I first joined the Air Corps and I knew I would eventually go overseas. As time went on, we had less and less real hope of knowing before we left. Information like that leaked out only as unfounded rumor, for which the Army is notorious. Then one afternoon we had a surprise. There was a plane near the field, and it sounded like a B-24, but we couldn't see it at first. Then someone saw it reflecting its color in the sky.

"Hey! There it is! Look, it's kinda pinkish -- flesh-colored! Brother! I know where we're goin' now! The Sahara Desert!"

There was no other explanation worth listening to. The two planes that came in that day were a dull pink, instead of the usual green, and the bellies were a bluish-purple. The next few days planes came in two or three at a time. A designated pilot signed for his ship after checking its equipment, and the ferry pilot took the receipt. Ed got the fourth one, and together we checked it over thoroughly and made several test flights. It was a tremendous thrill to practically own and be responsible for so great a machine worth $300,000. When it proved to have a weak fuel pump on one engine, the whole crew turned out to assist in changing it.

At the time our pink B-24's started arriving at our field about July 1, 1942, most of the co-pilots had been flying AT-6s (a single engine training plane) in the flying schools three months before and were now at their fourth field since graduation. The pilots had had about three additional months since school, but had done only a meager amount of flying. Some of that had been in twin-engine planes. Thompson's first night landing, and the only one until we were in combat, was made during our brief stay at Albuquerque. After we were safely down, he told me that it had been his first. I think they heard my gulp in the control tower.

Because we were desperately needed overseas and there were no combat-experienced men to train us, our preparation was far less than that of crews who trained six months to a year later. The combat teams barely knew each other, and had flown almost no formation together. We had no idea how close we would come to the enemy and were teaching ourselves to throw knives and axes. We did not think it possible that we would never see the enemy face to face in over a year in combat. I had never fired a sidearm or army rifle. We <u>did</u> have a fair knowledge of our airplane equipment, but we had never been briefed nor had we flown on a simulated mission. All officers were second lieutenants, except for one first lieutenant, and a doctor and commanding officer who were captains. Sturgis became a major just before we left.

Eleven men were assigned to go in our plane. In addition to the four officers, were Sgt. Adamowski, the engineer, a Polish boy of nineteen who was in charge of the enlisted crew -- that is, all but Sgt. Taylor who "submitted to no man, by God!" Taylor was a short stocky blond of twenty-two or three who had run away from home. He was a loveable tough kid with a lurching swagger, more pronounced at some times than others. He had joined the Army and had been stationed in Panama. Of that much I'm certain. I hesitate to set down as fact any of the many other tales he told at one time or another. At any rate, he was a tough soldier of the peacetime Army and served as a very capable tail gunner on our crew. Ed and I wanted both "Adam" and Taylor with us, but they were capable of spontaneously punchy speech, some of which had already blown between them. A good deal of reconciling had to be done before Taylor would fall in line with the dictate that the engineer, though younger and with a shorter army career, should be in charge of the entire crew.

"Hell, Lieutenant," Taylor once said, "I got more time in the pay line than that guy has in the chow line!"

In spite of his gruffness toward other enlisted men, Taylor's attitude toward the officers was excellent, and he always greeted us with a salute and smile even under the most informal conditions. When we pointed out that he had hurt himself frequently by being "busted" because of his own acts, he agreed to stick with our crew, because he felt we were really interested in him.

The assistant engineer and waist gunner was Sgt. Tony Filipo, a tall thin Italian. The radio operator was a pleasant boy of nineteen and the most intelligent man on the crew.

He had a beautiful soft red hair and was named Chadwick. Burns, a non-entity, was his assistant and a waist gunner. In addition to this combat crew were the chief crew, M/Sgt. Weeks, and the squadron Engineer Officer, Tucker.

Before it was time for us to leave, three ships had gained names. One was "Little Amber," one was "Alice the Goon," and looking forward to the results of its mission, another pink ship was called "Rosie Wrecked 'Em." Swetland painted a picture of an "Eager Beaver" on our ship, and so labeled it.

On the morning of July 11, when the first ten ships took off and assembled in formation, we knew only two things: that we would land next at Morrison Field, West Palm Beach, and that the color of our planes suggested the Sahara Desert. As we left the ground, I looked down and saw a big Buick on the edge of the road at the field, and something white moved in the black frame of the window, only vaguely lighted by the early morning sun. Swetland's mother was saying goodbye to a priceless son in his fighting ship snouted with a .50 caliber guns.

Within an hour we were lined up on a strip at Morrison Field. In two days, four planes returned to Tampa to have some work done. They were not too well put together, and the pilot had not accepted one, because a great number of rivets were loose in the wing structures.

On July 16th, we returned to Morrison were briefed on our forthcoming flight, and were issued personal equipment: a .45 automatic and holster for each officer, Springfield rifles for the crew, mosquito netting for our sleeping bags (which we already had), head netting for night wear, limp suede mosquito boots, dark glasses, flashlights, and many other articles of flying clothes. Our ships were loaded with spare parts even to an extra tire we could barely get into the bomb bay. Our gross load was above what was considered the absolute safe maximum. At 5:30, just as we were ready to eat and go to the hotel in town, we were told to get some sleep and report at our planes at 12:30. Takeoff was 0200 (2 a.m.). We unrolled our luxurious down bedrolls that we had been told to leave behind, but following Major Sturgis' example, had kept, and stretched out on them to sleep by the plane until midnight. Many times we were glad we had disobeyed orders and brought those bulky bedrolls.

Although for three weeks we had known we were to leave the United States, it was only this last evening that men showed signs of uneasiness. From our point of view, we were like Magellan or Columbus starting off into the unknown world. The mere fact we had by now seen our destination on a map didn't improve the situation worth a damn.

There was none of the usual rowdiness and kidding and swearing that always flowed as boisterously as beer on Saturday night, but there was a feeling of restlessness elation. You could tell by the smiling lines around the men's eyes even when they talked soberly that they felt both fear of the unknown and an excited desire for it. Perhaps the most remarkable picture was that of Taylor and Adam being friends. They sat cross-legged in front of the nose wheel in the semidarkness while Taylor, with fatherly gruffness, told about his eighteen months in Panama -- what the jungles and the towns and the people were like. I'm sure the youthful Adam was reassured by the prideful enthusiasm of our tail gunner

"Is that you, Lt. Gilbert?" asked Taylor with his New England accent. "I just been tellin' Adam here about Panama. You ever been out of the country?"

"No," I admitted. "This is my first time."

"Why, Lt. Gilbert," the little man rumbled, "I ran away from home when I was fifteen. Me and the old man didn't get along so good. I was really a devil, I guess. Me an' another guy used to go out with a gang an' drink, an' I was alla' time ditchin' school. This other kid an' me had a cabin we use t'stay at when my old man was huntin' fer me. He wanted me t'work in the garage with him, but I got tired of that stuff. I ain't seen my folks or wrote 'em for three yee-ahs."

"Don't they even know you transferred to the Air Corps and are going over?" I asked, not quite sure how much truth I was hearing.

"Naw," he said, looking down and growing quiet. I sensed pride and regret and was determined his folks should get a letter when we reached our destination.

Before my mind would give in to sleep that night in the States, it insisted on mulling just what we, as individuals, were leaving behind to see or never see again. That "never" scared me. It sounded very permanent.

My chief concern was my mother, whom I had sent north a few days before. I know I was the most important thing in her life. She had relatives, but no husband for comfort. Mother had an unbounded interest in everything that happened in the world. I think she would have liked to be co-pilot, though she was sixty-five years old. It would be up to me to bring the world to her through my letters. As for girls, I was starting from scratch. My engagement had just been broken, and I was beginning to realize that I felt more relieved than sad.

Ed's mother and father worked at an oil well in Texas, and I know that Ed felt a great respect for his mother. I felt sure there was no girl he was deeply attached to.

I had met Swetland's mother and knew that there were several girls he was interested in, but not seriously. Since his mother had just lost her husband, she would have a great deal of loneliness to overcome in Paul's absence.

Gimble who was particularly close to his dad, just moaned about leaving girls -- he didn't specify which one.

At that time, I knew almost nothing about the background of the crew, except for Taylor's conversation that evening. All the men were twenty-three years old or less; Adamowski, the engineer, was the youngest – nineteen, and he and Filipo were from Pennsylvania. Chadwick was from a little town in Montana. No one had a job he minded leaving in order to join the Air Corps.

The control tower operator sounded as though he knew the secret of our destination when two o'clock drew near. It was the tone he used. The words were always the same; "806 cleared to taxi for south takeoff." And Ed tried to give a casual "806, Roger" as he released the brakes and we lumbered out, the nose majestically bowing up and down. A B-24 is a clumsy-looking bug when squatting on its landing gear, but "806 taking off!" - our five minute interval had elapsed and our ship gained speed to the roar of its engines, slipped through blackness between the two rows of light dots, and lifted smoothly above the red runway end lights to become a thing of graceful flight. Behind were the lighted barracks area, and then the brighter red, blue, and white lights of West Palm Beach. On the left, the revolving beacon slowly swung around and grew dim.

The rest of the night we flew until in the grayness of dawn we passed over the rugged green mountains and narrow valleys of Haiti. Four or five hours later we sighted the coast of Venezuela and turned eastward to pick up our approach channel to Waller Field, Trinidad. As we overflew the harbor at Port of Spain, we saw a large convoy of camouflaged ships encircled by moving white threads of water that trailed the ever-frantic PT boats. Here, two complementary parts of a war team were passing, and with a sense of unreality we identified ourselves with this grim scene below.

After landing, and stopping only to arrange the order of guards between the enlisted men and ourselves, we set our course for the Officers' Club which stood high on stilts among the few other buildings, it being standard operating procedures (S.O.P.) for Army officers to find their club among the first things at a new field. The atmosphere in the single room of the building seemed stiff at first in the presence of the few neatly groomed officers, but as our men grew in numbers we felt more at ease and enjoyed ourselves at the bar and the Ping-Pong table. After supper, we were briefed by Waller Field personnel for the next leg of our flight, and I, for one, was bedded down and netted in soon thereafter under the wing of the plane. One by one during the night the crewmembers sampling the social and spirituous component of the post, scuffed back to their "sacks." (as the sleeping bags were called). Liquor set a good trap for sleep, and it was used freely. Some of the men took rooms in the barracks, but there seemed to be less trouble involved in sleeping by the plane.

When we took off the next morning, the steam of the jungle was condensed over the treetops in a fluffy layer that was occasionally torn by the green spike of a taller tree. We flew in three separate elements of three planes each. Our element stayed at 8000 feet off the South American coast to avoid the cumulus clouds building up over the land. We passed over Devil's Island, reached the Oyapok River at 11:00 a.m. and turned southward to Belem. The Oyapok had snaking bands of red, tan, and green mud with patterns of clear water where fresh streams emptied in.

The mouth of the Amazon was like an open sea, and was far less picturesque than the Oyapok. We lost altitude into turbulence and thundershowers, and finding the Pan-American field just outside Belem, we circled and landed.

We had heard stories of sabotage on those South American airfields, so when our bomb bay doors rumbled open, the barefooted Brazilian laborers who had promptly arrived to refuel us found themselves face to face with eleven unsmiling foreigners carrying .45 automatics, Tommy guns, and Springfield rifles. There was a brief moment of intense silence. Then with a babble of Portuguese, our helpers climbed aboard their little gas truck and chugged it desperately back to their point of departure across the field. It was an hour before they could be persuaded to return.

We left our own guard on the plane that night, and the rest of us were taken in to the Grande Hotel via the wildest taxi ride wilder than even a Los Angeles passenger could imagine! We sped down red earth roads lined with people, huts, and jungle; swirled around sharp corners, down bumpy brick streets, and constantly plowed our way through swarms of people who seemed to open a path just ahead of the bumper. The driver casually steered with one hand and methodically bumped the horn with the other.

Downtown the streets were cobblestone lined with buildings of weather stained pastel. Ed and I shared our accommodations and had our meals for about $3.00 apiece, or sixty Milreis. The food was good, as was the beer, but the hotel was quite crowded and, for the first time, we heard very little English spoken. After dinner we went to our small high-ceilinged room furnished solely with two beds covered with white mosquito netting. In an adjoining room, there was a toilet, bath tub, electric water heater, and -- embarrassment, oh, embarrassment -- a douche bowl which seemed to be standard equipment.

Word began to circulate that there were several nightspots on a little street around the corner, but the nightspots turned out to be well-patronized houses of "female industry". The ages of the girls ranged from about 14 on up. I learned that half the girls lived in outlying districts and saved their money for this trip to town when they rented a room from the madam. They were there for their pleasure, and if the customers were very nice enough there was no charge. The places served beer at no abnormal cost, and there were music and dancing partners for those not otherwise inclined. Such a place seemed to be considered by the townspeople we met to afford a fairly legitimate evening's entertainment.

The next day we flew to Natal, Brazil, where a small number of Americans were frantically building a post that could service the ever-increasing flow of American planes overseas. There were no more than four buildings in all, one of which was a rather sad excuse for a mess hall. When I came back through fourteen months later, it had long since been expanded about twenty times and looked like the important installation it was. When we parked our planes in the hot sun and blowing sand on that July 20th, by far the more important part of the field belonged to the Germans, who still had German and Italian planes and personnel everywhere. Our American neutrals had not yet seen fit to evict the Axis. We were surprised that the United States tolerated their presence at this strategic base on our supply route.

I thought this might be my last chance to be civilized, so that night I slept under a sheet; all the base could furnish us, to go with their cots. By morning I was shivering like a crisp leaf. The next day I bargained with some laborers for their facas or salva vidas. These were beautifully graceful daggers with extremely sharp points and colored bone handles. After studying the men, I was quite sure they didn't use them for opening letters as I was intending to do.

The laborers themselves were generally short and thin, but all variations of features and shades of brown or yellow were apparent. Some of the men looked like direct descendants of the Aztecs, while others had finely-cut European features. The main mark of similarity was their clothing and bare-feet. The trousers were of loose-fitting cotton, usually white, supported by a rope or cloth tied at the waist. The shirts were loose, too, and tended to be more colorful than the trousers. Another thing they all had in common was a gleam in their eyes when they pulled out their knives to show me. These were carried in the sleeve or inside the shirt at chest or waist level.

Major Sturgis knew his B-24. Most of the trans-Atlantic traffic stopped at the Ascension Island for refueling. The island was about two-thirds of the way across and slightly off course, but even with our terrific load, the Major was sure that we could make it all the way to Accra, Gold Coast, in one hop. I guess he had been testing fuel consumption quite accurately on our previous runs. We accepted the Major's judgment and took off at 6:30 that night.

From my point of view, I was glad it was dark. It seemed more like just another night flight instead of pointing myself out over so darn much water. The previous night two British pilots went down with their Hudsons only a few miles out. Now that I think back, that was the kindergarten course in combat -- starting out on something the outcome of which was uncertain.

We flew at 9000 feet to avoid the cumulus clouds that would be building up over water at night and low enough that we didn't have to use oxygen, because we had none in our tanks. For the first few hours, while we used gas out of our bomb bay tanks, the ship mushed badly, so that we had to pull quite a bit of power to maintain safe flying speed. That worried us because of the accompanying high fuel consumption, but as the tanks gave up their fuel, the ship would level out in flight, the airspeed increased, and we could reduce power. We flew on the autopilot, and once or twice

Ed dozed, but I couldn't quite relax enough to make it. We had hot coffee available all the time and ate from our store of canned beans, sardines, peaches, salmon, and corned beef.

Swetland was the busiest man that night. The whole weight of whether or not we reached our destination before the fuel gave out was on him, and he felt it. This was his first long celestial navigation mission since school, and this one was "for keeps" -- there is no alternate airport in the mid-Atlantic -- so he took some phenomenal number of shots with his octant that night. When the Southern Cross became visible, as it does only in the southern hemisphere, he called us up on the interphone to remark about it, and signed off with an embarrassed little laugh that meant he might have shown a little too much enthusiasm about something we weren't interested in. But he was wrong. We gazed at it for quite a while. There was nothing original about my thoughts. I considered how far from home we were getting, and wondered what the future had in wait for us in this strange part of the world.

Dawn came at about 4:00 a.m. Natal time, and at 6:30 we were flying parallel to and south of the African coast in patches of fog and low overcast. We went down to 2000 feet, and when Swetland said we were an hour overdue at the coast, we turned northeast, flying through bank after bank of fog. Each successive fog line looked like the shoreline until we were close to it. Finally we sighted land at 7:30, and identified it as the Ivory Coast -- French territory. At Takkeraddi (British) we flew too close to the harbor and suddenly found a sleek Spitfire on one wing and a deadly Beaufighter on the other. We waved. The pilots waved back, stuck with us for a few minutes, and then left. At one place, we flew over a point of land, and I remember seeing the villages as red splotches in the green of the forests. The huts were made of the soil and could hardly be seen even as close as we were. The water was dotted with outrigger canoes carrying latine sails. The boats seemed to be engaged in fishing.

Over the radio, we heard the Accra station calling one of our ships that had crossed the coast up north of the bulge not far from Vichy French territory. They were trying to give the ship a bearing to fly. We finally sighted the sunken boat we had been briefed to look for as an identification of Accra harbor, turned to the field, and landed at 11:00 Accra time after fifteen hours and twenty-five minutes of flight. A few minutes after us came Major Sturgis, whom we had passed traveling at a snail's pace. In order to conserve fuel, he had had his power cut back so far it seemed almost possible to count the revolutions of his propellers. The ship we had heard on the radio came in an hour later, and one of its engines cut from lack of gas while he was taxiing to his parking lane.

This was a Pan-American Airlines station with good barracks, good food -- especially coffee -- American style, which we had begun to miss. The black boys who worked there made an impression on all of us, because of their willingness, courtesy, and varying styles of English speech. But the men guarding our planes, who wrapped themselves in blankets or dilapidated trench coats and wielded their rifles and bayonets in a business-like way, looked coldly ferocious, so we didn't go to our planes after dark. They were noted for their confusion about the sequence of pulling the trigger and saying "Halt."

Ed and I had a brief stroll through the streets of Accra, and became initiated to the unfamiliar filth we were to see everywhere. The English homes were mostly of brick, and their grounds were very comfortable looking, but in the business district it was quite different. The deep cement gutters of the hard-surfaced streets seemed to be the latrines and general removal mediums, while dried fish were displayed for sale on the streets themselves. The barefooted natives, of all sizes and statures, were usually wrapped in great pieces of uproariously colored print calico--flaming pink, purple, green--with head windings, scarcely turbans, of the same. Big loads rocked gracefully on the heads of the women, and occasionally from under an extra wrapping of cloth at the small of a woman's back a fuzzy little black head peeked out of its rumble-seat sling where this fragile cargo rode easily just above the tremendous motion of two enormous hips.

One wrinkled old lady, when she saw that I was taking pictures, danced in front of the camera with such an exhilarated look on her face, that a little boy became much more intrigued with her than with the white "sa'ibs". However, when the camera clicked, she immediately became business-like and stretched out a palm. There were occasional giant black men that we saw more of in Khartoum. Their garb was a muslin nightshirt with broad enough sleeves to permit rapid access to a short and vicious dagger strapped to the forearm.

In taking a short cut between two main streets, Ed and I passed down a narrow dirt alley that made me so sick I wanted to hold my breath, close my eyes, and run. There were listless old black people meagerly wrapped in filthy cloth, eyes sunken, toothless, and black hair gone gray with filth as well as age. They sat in the dust at the edge of a shallow, sewage-cluttered ditch sucking on dirty pieces of dried fish. Or just holding themselves braced in an upright position by clasping their hands on their emaciated knees. In this position the dry, wrinkled skin on their chest could come and go a little easier with breathing. The naked children, unlike the ones we had just seen jigging and chanting a block or so away, were sucking on beads or kicking at lumps in the dust, not moving their pot-bellied bodies with much enthusiasm. And the dogs were third best. Covered with sores and thin from starvation, they wandered along the gutter area picking out occasional morsels to see if they were edible. The smell of the whole street was the summation of everything vulgar that is either flushed away or carried off from where people live at home. The heat of the sun subdued the general uprising of odor, but from the damp and shaded corners the smells of decay and excrement crept out retchingly.

I thought, "How can people live like this?" But the answer was easy -- "Because they have to." I had seen destitute human beings, but never starving ones. So this is what the papers mean when they say people are starving in Russia or Greece or France.

I have never been starved and know no one who has, but from that day the word lost its all-inclusive ambiguity. Starvation means filth and disease and loss of interest in the manner or purpose of life. Starved people are concerned only with being alive. How can we accuse people of not making progress when they are starving?

Our weather forecast between Accra and Khartoun sounded good, so we took off at 5:30 p.m. We hit an overcast off the end of the runway and flew in it for eight or nine hours. When we tried to go above the stuff so Swetland could take some shots on the stars, we went as high as 17,000 feet without oxygen and then hit icing that began to coat the plane. We came back down to 10,000 feet, but the air was violently rough. This was particularly dangerous with our heavy load. Knowing that we were not due to reach any mountains until after daylight, we went down to about 3000 feet and flew in smooth air, but terrific rain.

At dawn, the skies were clear, and the rains made great washes of the red wastes of the Sudan with its scattered clumps of brush. Our radio compass, tuned to El Fasher, told us when we passed by, and Swetland gave us a new heading to make us hit below the junction of the Blue and White Niles.

Wadi Seidna field near Khartoum was almost obscured by the dust, but we landed, taxied to a dispersion area, and parked not far from the meager Sudanese thatched hut with a rude corral of thorn around it. We had barely cut the engines, when an animated black skeleton stomped out of the hut and, hesitating to come too close to the big pink bird, assailed us from beyond the wingtip. All the while he pointed to the ground between the rear of our plane and his hut, motioning the plane forward.

Finally Adamowski, the Engineer, got it. "Oh, hey, d'guy wants us t'get off his pat'. Dat sharp rock must have hurt his bare feet when he walks aroun'".

Sure enough, a path was just barely discernable, but we were too anxious for breakfast to start up the engines again, so he stomped back to his hut, probably to fall asleep while the two women and the children within his little stockade continued at whatever they were doing in the shade of a scrub tree.

During the course of the next hour, the rest of our planes straggled in. I believe we were the second to land. We were gazing with strained eyes at the southwest horizon and usually spotted each plane before we heard it. One by one they circled the field to the left, and upon being identified and receiving permission to land, the black disks that were tires would seem to fall in slow motion out of the wing nacelles and the structure of the landing gear would flop into a vertical position as the long slender wings tilted into a bank. Each plane would nose toward the earth in a descending turn that straightened out for a few brief seconds as the pink bomber lined up with the runway and cautiously eased onto it. When close above the ground, the plane almost disappeared in the dust stirred up by the numerous P-40's that were running up their engines at scattered points. The usual screech of the big tires gaining instantaneous acceleration upon contact with the ground was muffled by the sand that lay over everything, but behind the wheels tight funnel-shaped clouds of sand trailed back into the general dust. As the brakes were applied, the low-squatting fuselage would tip forward not too gracefully on the nose wheel and the twin rudders would lift upward like a bird tipping its tail to balance on a small twig.

By the time the Pan-American bus had collected us and hauled us to the hangar at the corner of the fields, only nine ships had landed.

"Looks like one of the boys is a little late," I said.

Now that we were relaxed in the safety of the ground, it didn't occur to me that one plane and its crew would never arrive.

By noon, when it was established that Richardson's crew was missing, we wanted to take all the planes and search, but we were told that search planes would be sent out from Kano and El Fasher. We all felt guilty sitting down to a good meal when Richardson, Kerkin, Sterns, and Doc Willis might need help desperately. Although we had been achingly hungry a little while before, no one ate very much and the conversation was low. I was doing the kind of thinking you do when you look at a dream you're having and try to decide if it really is a dream. I knew this wasn't, and my mind turned to sights of battered men groaning on the hot sand amid the annihilation of an airplane and though I directed my thoughts to someone else, they would creep back when I relaxed. This was the sudden loss of men we all knew and liked at a time when we hadn't thought about such a possibility. I knew by the solemn faces of the others at the table, that they were thinking the same thoughts, and with those thoughts was a little cold fear that it might have been any one of us. At a moment like that you realize how preciously fragile and un-renewable life is, and unless you are utterly unselfish, you make a new effort to hang on to your own identity more tenaciously than ever. What would it be like to face a shooting enemy and be concerned with staying alive?

It was two weeks before we heard that Richardson had crashed many miles from Kano. When the party reached the wreckage, eleven graves were found. Someone else had gotten there first to bury them.

Had the plane iced up? Had it run out of gas? Had lack of oxygen at high altitude caused Richardson to lose control? The path to death remains unmarked for those who would inquire and return.

To this day, I can see the expression that must have been on Doc Willis' face when he became aware that death in an airplane was whirling closer. Doc, as a Flight Surgeon, had gone on altitude test hops with me, and I had frequently seen his square face and blue eyes in terror when the plane made a movement he didn't understand. It was impossible not to picture the horror he must have known before he crashed.

When our footlockers finally arrived three months later, we opened Doc's and found only a pair of shorts, his dress blouse, a raincoat, and a pair of tennis shoes. Before word of his death had reached his wife, she had sent pictures of their new baby that Doc had been so adoringly gruff with, and the sight of those brought new lumps to our throats.

Wadi Seidna was primarily a British post, although Pan-American maintained a station there, and the permanent stone buildings that were assigned as our transient quarters smacked intriguingly of outpost garrisons and far-away lands. The cheapest of manual labor was evident by the large number of black Mohammedans who loitered around as servants. They were clothed in the usual muslin nightshirts, but with the addition of braced red bands at their waists to signify that they were attached to the staff. On their heads were red tarbrooshes, and the men padded silently about on their broad bare feet.

The building was in the shape of an open square with an inside verandah, and three times during the main part of the day, these black men would step silently, one by one, into the center grass plot, where on their knees they whispered passages of the Koran and bowed their heads to the earth. The strict Muslim must wash his hands and feet before each of his five daily prayers, but when out in the desert where water is scarce, he may cleanse himself with dust instead.

At the washroom at the rear of the building, there were no plumbing facilities for toilets, in spite of the long row of modern washbowls and mirrors. It was the duty of the servants to remove the jars and pots of the latrine booths at regular intervals and to deposit the contents at some distance from the buildings in a pit provided for the purpose.

That night one of the usual poker games developed. The number of players varied from four to nine during the first two hours, and then settled down at seven. The stakes weren't high, but everyone had fun, whether playing or kibitzing. Thompson proved to be keen at the game, and almost seemed to have a sixth sense for raising or dropping. He won $40 that night. Later, when I used to come up to him at poker or crap games, I found out how he was faring by asking, "Well, Ed, do you want me to hold your head or your money? And usually it was his money. I remember thinking how well off I was to be teamed up with someone who was so phenomenally lucky. Other men sometimes lost tremendous amounts -- as high as $1,000 -- but if Ed lost, the sum was small and he more than regained it at the next game.

If life in battle was like the roll of dice, I would stick with Ed and survive on his luck. But wasn't there a belief that even winning gamblers lost in the end! I didn't know, and my mind was not at rest.

The following night, there was a party of some kind at a little place in Khartoum, about 30 miles away. Most of us went in early to see the town first. The western section of town looked as though it were filled with every sort of rough character that would like to cause trouble for some future Kitchener. The streets led between high walls of brown dried mud on which cakes of dung were plastered to dry for use as fuel. Each cake bore the imprint of a hand. There was little else between the walls, except the swarms of black Sudanese men and a few women with their camels or donkeys. Occasionally there was a bicycle which withdrew to the rough edge of the road at the approach of the airport bus. Somehow, these people all managed to look murderous.

In the center of town was a streetcar line, a few attractive shops, many nondescript ones, and nearby was a particularly picturesque building was a Moslem school of religion. Along the river was a shady road with some grand and substantial English homes and clubs.

Quite a crowd gathered at the dance atop the café. The large assemblage of British and American officers and enlisted men gawked at the few English girls and nurses. The English beer and Australian ale were good and cold, which fact we appreciated no end, because we were beginning to find that wholesale refrigeration had ceased to exist. The beer ran out after a while and gin and brandy were the main reserves.

I soon became tired, leaving Ed at the dance, I went back to the field, plowed past a noisy crap game, and went to bed. Hours later, Ed came in with a dozen or more ivory trinkets -- elephants, necklaces, pins, bookmarks, etc. He had bargained with a weary ivory vendor, one who had followed us, barking extravagant prices during the day. Now, whether the ivory wallah had unloaded his wares at half his normal profit, receiving only five times their worth, or actually been blown into confusion by Ed's inebriated harangue, I make no venture, but if an American really bested the East in a bargain, the fact should immediately be recorded. Anyway, it was with amazement and no memory as he surveyed all his purchases next morning.

After breakfast, we were to take off for a formation flight up the Nile to our base -- just where, we didn't know. The flight that morning was an unhappy event. As the morning progressed, the air grew rougher until it was almost impossible not only to stay in formation, but to be near another ship. It was the most sickening rollercoaster I have ever been on. Our ship wallowed 500 feet up and then 500 feet down, and all the other planes were doing the same thing in a dreamy motion that belied how hard the pilots worked and sweated to keep their craft in any semblance of proximity. Whether from the motion alone, or aided by the mixture of beverages consumed the night before, all but one or two persons in the entire flight were sick to their stomachs and had little appreciation for the sights they flew over. I had been sick at breakfast and had no more to contribute.

The great north-flowing Nile River wound for hundreds of miles through pure sand without so much as a sign of vegetation. The sand was broken in places by hills or ranges of hills that looked like piles of rough slag the desert sands were ashamed of and were trying to hide. Suddenly patches of cultivated green began to show. The areas spread, and soon we were following a lane of green that bordered the river and ended on either side in a razor-fine line where it met the sand of the desert. At Cairo, we turned northeast to cross Great Bitter Lake and the Suez Canal, and skirt the blue corner of the Mediterranean. Just beyond the haze northwest of Cairo was the El Alamein line. Reaching the Palestine shore, we passed the gleaming white modern city of Tel-Aviv next to its ancient dark neighbor, Jaffa.

Just a few miles short of Haifa, we turned to go over the low range of hills and drop down into the valley sheltering our field, landing into the glaring red sunset.

There were large stone revetments and crews of Limies waiting for us. When the plane was swung around tail toward the revetment and the motors were cut, we had the first real meeting with our allies. Their officer put the men to work pushing the plane backward by hand, groaning the effort –uniting phrase: "All right, Lods! All t'gether now! Twooo and six! That's it, Lods! Once agin -- twooo and six! -- as though that were to be the value of their effort. At last we were with the British.

So ended nine swift days of transition. A great portion of the world had been changed from colors and names on a map and descriptions in a book to streets I could walk on. Languages that were never real in print -- Portuguese and African tongues -- became garbled sounds in rhythm. The almost soundless squelch of a camel's calloused foot on sand had never before come alive, even in movies. Even smells that had never been attempted in print—and it was easy to know why. Smells that grab the pit of the stomach, and twisted like a pair of pliers. Smell of all the filth of humans and animal and decay, and people living amid it who had known little else. And sights! Little black children in all their hungry filth jigging in unconcerned rhythm to the strange music they hummed. The Nile, the Mediterranean Sea, the Suez, and the Soudan where peoples now extinct made history an incomprehensible measure of time ago. These parts of he world were coming alive in my mind.

And eleven men were dead.

There is a fundamental law of physics states that energy can neither be created nor destroyed. Look at this squadron over the shoulder of that law. I doubt if the men in those planes would ever have had the will and the money to displace themselves from America to Palestine. It took the energy of a war to do it. Once displaced, the men saw people and places and conditions fomenting a sudden love for their own land and sympathy in understanding other lands. There is the foundation for the platform of world peace. For that nine days of other men's awakening, eleven men gave up the energy of life.

The achievement of world peace will need tremendous energy, as does the waging of war. The energy of the millions who die must be well used by the millions who live.

Chapter II

COMBAT

We were given three days to make ourselves and our ship ready for combat. "Eager Beaver" was in good mechanical shape and mainly needed to shave the spare parts and the bomb bay racks removed so that the bombs could be put in. When this was done, we settled ourselves into quarters which were British double-walled tents pitched on a low hill. The toilet facilities consisted of two six-hole circular privies and two water faucets with long wooden benches to place washbowls on. Later, Arab laborers installed four open-air showers.

On one side of our hill was a Russian Jewish cooperative called "Gevat", and half a mile on the other was a larger settlement called "Nahillil", which was arranged in a circle of cottages with cultivated strips of radiating outward -- a beautiful landmark to identify the field by.

The field, called "Ramat-David" after a third cooperative which shared the hilltop with us, was really not ready for us, so the messing problem was difficult at first. Since we had no ground personnel of our own, we had to queue up with the British enlisted men whose messes are noted for their luxurious cuisine. Breakfast consisted always of sweet tea, which was good, thick slices of bread cooked in sugar water, and served with eggless custard. The other meals were corned beef or beans with tea, and slabs of breads with canned butter that the heat turned into thin cheese. We began losing weight and used some emergency rations we had in the plane.

Two men from each crew guarded the planes at night. Gimble and I guarded together one night in the bright moonlight with a tommygun across our knees and our .45s handy. There were small African guards who scuffed by in their heavy hobnailed shoes during the night. They would come up to ask for cigarettes by pretending to suck on one, and invariably asked what time it was so they could see our watches. About midnight, we were startled by the sound of explosions at a distance, and learned the following day that an Axis submarine was near the harbor at Haifa and that the British had dropped depth charges. There was an oil refinery within shelling distance of the water as well as a harbor full of cargo boats and tankers. Gimble talked about some girls he had been living riotously with in Miami. I listened and grinned. After 1:00 A.M. we found it hard to stay awake so we took turns dozing and patrolling the revetment.

It was interesting to watch the Arab laborers who were still building runways and taxi strips on the airfield. Some of them made little straw lean-tos and slept and ate there on the field. At night they sometimes sat in small groups in the dark and one or two would sing whiningly through this nose, as the rest chanted a chorus. They laughed throatily when they finished. I wondered what American song would compare with theirs -- and if they could be printable.

During the day the boys and men and a few women broke large limestone rocks into small chunks. They used hammers or smashed the rocks against each other then fitted the pieces together so that a steamroller could crush them into a smooth surface. The men wore dilapidated shoes with the back of the shoe folded under the heel of the foot to form a slipper. Their trousers were white or black cotton, fitting closely from the ankle to the knee, and then blossoming out in a profusion of cloth that sagged down from where it was tied at the waist. I have been told in the greatest sincerity that some Arabs who believe women are too unworthy of the great honor, expect Mohammed will one day be reborn through the posterior orifice of a male body. Perhaps this accounts for the trouser style. At least, they were made to keep out sand and give maximum coolness and freedom of movement. The shirts were of white cotton, and over all was a long coat with a sash at the waist, into which the front corners of the coat were lifted and tucked to keep them out of the way when working. Their headdress was the traditional cloth that reached to the shoulders and east held in place by a ring of soft cord fitted the crown of the head. The Arabs frequently left their work to stand and look at us with a stare that would be considered rude at home, but apparently had no such connotation for them. The boys could speak English, and one, with much enthusiasm and diligence tried to exact a fabulous price from me before I was allowed to take a picture of his striking father. The father smilingly looked out of he corner of his eye as he continued to put stones in place while his son called over his shoulder in Arabic the progress of the deal, the latter never letting his keen brown eyes leave my face. I put the money -- a few mils (125 mils is about $1.00) -- into the hand of the father instead of the boy's outstretched hand, and after taking the picture, found out all that he really wanted was a good razor to tackle his beard with. This I later furnished.

The clothing of the women seemed to consist of several layers of loose cotton dresses and a longer head cloth, part of which served formerly as a veil. Now it trailed down their backs. They almost always wore heavy silver bracelets and anklets, an easy way to carry wealth. It is not easy to get a good look at their faces, for although only a few women wear veils, they turn their faces away from strangers. Past the age of about 30, an Arab woman of the poor class begins to look old and toil-worn, for she does many heavy duties, the most picturesque of which is the carrying of tremendous loads on her head.

We tried to learn a few Arabic and Hebrew words from little books we bought and this pleased them a great deal. Perhaps the only one that I will never forget is the Hebrew word "shalom" which means "peace" and is their word of both greeting and departure. When present day Arabs have a dispute about one of their words, they take the question to a Bedouin of the desert tribes whose language is still pure and unchanged from earliest times. There is a similarity between Arabic and Hebrew, but I believe that Hebrew more nearly resembles the ancient language of the Bedouins than it does the Arabic of the coast.

One night Swetland and I went to a Russian Movie at the Gevat settlement as ranking guests. The show, which was held in the open and projected on a screen nailed to the side of a building, was a good Gestapo story with titles in French, German, and Hebrew. The sound was in Russian. Albert, a member of the "Pioneers" (an auxiliary Palestine Army serving with the British), translated into English for us when we couldn't follow the German. Albert stood on guard for seven hours straight with little to eat. I know that more than once an English gun crew there was given a can of bully beef to last three men a day, and, I'm sorry to say, such treatment didn't help the feeling of the Jews for the British.

The next night I wandered into the settlement of Nahillil and found that ice-cold milk could be bought at the dairy. It was truly a fountain in the desert. I think I have never before nor since enjoyed milk so much. It was not pasteurized, but I gathered that their diseased cattle had been segregated. At any rate, I could not resist the cold milk. Anything chilled was suddenly at high premium in this country with scarce means of refrigeration.

Very few people in the settlement could speak English, except for several children who spoke it well, and so I was surprised to hear someone in front of the dairy say "Good evening." He was a pleasant little man named Moses, who, we learned after a few words, was in charge of the police. He insisted that when he went off duty at nine o'clock Lt. Garner and myself should go with him to his home. We thought that would be very kind of him and waited for until nine o'clock.

Another couple was living with him and his wife until their unpretentious white cottage, like this one, could be built. We enjoyed sitting outside at a table in the moonlight, drinking milk and eating fine apples, plums, and grapes picked from nearby. Garner knew only French and I only German, so there were two circles of conversation, with Moses and his wife, like good hosts, participating in each.

I learned about two features of the Jewish cooperative that I had not been familiar with. They used the system of trial marriage wherein a man and a woman could live and work their plot of land together until they decided to call it off or get married. If a child resulted, however, marriage was obligatory. The second feature was that many of the cooperatives used only communal property so that no one needed money of his own unless he was taking a vacation and left the community, whereupon he was given his portion.

After that night, I frequently walked into Nahillil to exercise my German with Moses, but I'm afraid he achieved more with his English. On the outskirts of town whose population was under 1,000, was a fairly modern dairy and agriculture school for girls, which taught them what they needed to know to be a good farmer's wives. One Saturday night Moses invited three of the girls and three of us to his house for a radio dance. It was rather an embarrassed gathering with too many language barriers, but we appreciated his effort. When I asked if they ever had any large dances, he shook his head and said that at large gatherings the Arabs sometimes slipped in and caused trouble. One time when we were talking about the green busses that rattled in and out of Haifa, he said: "You know, the Arab and Jewish busses used to be different colors, but the Arab busses started to dynamite the roads under our busses, so now all are green."

We had our first combat mission on August 1 and flew to Fayid Field near Great Bitter Lake to bomb up and be briefed. Major Kalberer, an American who had come with the heavy bomb group that arrived ahead of us, and who was now serving with the British at this advanced base, did most of the briefing. It was like the first day of flying school. He grinned as he said that nothing big was expected, but as an opening lesson, we were to bomb the enemy tank repair ground at Mersa Matruh. There would be some Wellingtons there at 8000 feet just ahead of us to light up the target, but the target wouldn't be hard to find because of the moonlit white appearance of a nearby salt lake. We were to go singly at 16,000 feet. We were instructed in the approach channels to this field, what flare signals to use, how to locate ourselves by blinking lights when we came back into the delta region, and told that if there were enemy planes here when we came back, we would be warned by a double red flare from the ground. Planes were given British designations of "C" for Charlie, "D" for Donald, "F" for Freddie, and so on. We had supper at the British officers' mess, and I curled up on the stone verandah for a snooze until time to go to the planes at midnight.

I didn't get much sleep. My mind wouldn't cooperate. It pictured everything from night fighters coming in unseen for the kill to a commendation for turning the tide of the war by our wiping out the enemy tank repair station. I dozed once or twice, then stumbled to the snub-nosed truck that took us through absolute darkness to our planes. How the driver found the plane I don't know. The enemy could be no more mystified by our secrecy than I was.

We followed directions to the letter, waited our turn for takeoff, and flew westward, gaining altitude. I was confused by the feeling that this was an ordinary night flight, but knowing we were flying over enemy-held land. As we turned to approach Matruh from the south, we strained our eyes into the blackness below the dome of stars. I was nervous and felt chilled where my spine was wet with perspiration. Chadwick was in his top turret just behind us, Taylor in the tail turret, Filipo and Burns were at the waist guns, and Swetland was peering over Gimble's shoulder trying to find a landmark where there was nothing.

Suddenly, in the near distance, red lines curved upward into the dark below us. I didn't realize immediately that I was seeing enemy tracers -- they were the first I had ever seen at night. Then there was a flash of light followed by several others. The Wellingtons were dropping their bombs -- we were right on time. Soon the coast showed up like a luminous line, and then there was a larger spot that would be the dry salt lake.

The bomb bay doors rumbled open and a cold breeze went by my legs. Gimble called "on course" over the interphone. Ed settled down to make the movement of the plane keep the indicator needle on his plane centered. I peered into blackness and sweated. The bomb release light flashed, and the horizon tipped to the left as we banked away to the right and lost altitude. That's all there was. Minutes of apprehension followed, but the night guarded us, and gradually we felt safe again. We saw nothing and heard nothing.

When Jerry finally answered Ed's questions over the interphone, he sounded vague: "Hell, Ed, I don't know if we did any good. There were flashes in the target area. I suppose they were our bombs. I've never seen a real bomb explode at night before."

Forty-five minutes later we saw a flashing light that Swetland identified as Burg El Arab, and he gave us our course home. Now that we knew just where we were in all this unintelligible blackness, we felt much more confident of ourselves.

The following night, we were sent over Tobruk to bomb the shipping in the harbor from 24,000 feet. It was a dark night and only two of eight planes found the target. One stumbled over the blacked-out town and suddenly found itself in the middle of bursting flak and brilliant flares. It quickly dumped its bombs and came home. We had to bring ours home without even seeing the target.

We tumbled into bed at dawn, after being interrogated about what we had seen and done. Six hours had scarcely ticked off, when we were awakened to go on another mission. We had just finished breakfast when someone else took our place, so we returned to our base in Palestine.

As a preamble to our third or fourth mission, Colonel Crom, who was in charge of Intelligence for the 9th. Air Force under General Brereton, put in an appearance before us at one of our briefings at Fayid. He wanted us to know just what part we were actually playing in the effort to knock Rommel out of Africa. He reviewed the push-pull war in which British under Wavell had captured Cyrenaica from the Italians in

February of 1941, lost it, captured it again from the Germans, and then were pushed back and besieged at Tobruck. They had held at Sollum until November of 1941, and then under the onslaught of armored columns of the Germans, which had even out-advanced their own airforce. They were pushed back to the present line at El Alamein.

In spite of the fact that the enemy was stretching his supply lines across the desert to a length of nearly 400 miles from Benghazi, they were shortened to only 150 miles, because he could get supplies into Tobruk. Aircraft was the best arm with which to destroy shipping, but the range of British ships from Malta flying eastward, and the range of British ships flying from Egypt flying westward still left a gap 75 to 100 miles wide where tankers, troopships, and freighters that started far up the Adriatic could come down the coast of Greece, jump to Crete, and thence across to Tobruk and Benghazi, hampered only by what few submarines could be put against them. It was in that sea lane that we were to be most important.

A long range Spitfire from Malta kept track of the enemy shipping as it originated and watched it down to Navarino Bay at Pylos on the west coast of Greece where our planes could make the first contact. From there the ships would either go to Candia Bay in Crete, or just skirt the Cretan coast and head out across the Mediterranean. They were fair game all the way. Sometimes they were escorted by destroyers or cruisers, but usually the main protection for the convoys or single ships would come from the pursuit aircraft based on Crete. For that reason, the Crete airfields would also be our targets.

"And," Colonel Crom went on, "your bombing won't stop when enemy ships have managed to reach port. You'll bomb the cargo at the docks themselves, bomb it in the warehouse or scattered dumps, and you may even have to bomb it on the road until it gets down to where shorter range planes can get a crack at it. General Montgomery is determined to drive the Germans back, and the most crucial item to destroy is their oil and gasoline. We know already that Rommel is hard pressed for the tanks, because he takes great pains to retrieve his damaged tanks, and when necessary haul them clear back to Mersa Natruh for repair."

The Colonel then told us what precautions were being maintained to retrieve any airmen on the desert or at sea. He gave each combat crew-member a map of the area we flew over. In looking at the map of the Sahara Desert, which we thought to be a great expanse of uninhabited sand, we saw hundreds of names.

"Don't be fooled by all the names on that map," he said. "The few that have water are in big print, and those may not have water the year round. Most of them are graves or monuments that you might have trouble recognizing if you were standing on them."

In addition to the map, he gave us minute compasses to steer us on the desert, and a sheet of parchment known as a "Blood Chit". There were two styles of compasses, the larger of which had two portions each looking like a regular black button when sewn on the clothing, but when put together one was the base and the other the moving top to the compass. The blood chit was for use incase we ran into or were picked up by the Arabs. The Arabs were running a shuttle service for both armies by returning men shot down in the desert, and the Americans were offering a reward of $20 in silver for each man brought back.

"This chit," Colonel explained, "is to make the Arabs aware of the fact that you are Americans. The Senoussi Arabs that Mussolini has tried to keep in his part of the desert by means of a 300 mile barbed wire fence have vowed to kill and torture any Italians they get hold of. They might get some Germans, too. Some of the Arabs are not too friendly to the British, although the offer of a reward seems to have soothed them somewhat, but people in this part of the world are still somewhat fond of Americans, so be sure you identify yourself as one." (The Senoussi did attack some Italians after we won Tunisia, and the British were forced to fire on them.)

The chit had a picture of an American Eagle, under which was the phrase: "I am an American. Take me to the nearest British post and you will be rewarded." Under each word were the sounds we were supposed to make as the Arabic equivalent. There were other words for water, food, etc.

Before leaving us, Col. Crom emphasized four things that meant life or death on the desert: rest during the day, walk during the night, drink your water slowly, avoid exposure to the sun.

"The British are continually getting a large percent of their airmen back from the desert. It may take months to come out on camel back. If at all possible, stick by your plane for two days and give our air and ground patrols a chance to find you. We want you back, and we will do our utmost to help you. Good luck, and I'll be seeing you again."

I think the first month of operations was the busiest, for we put in ninety combat hours. Two other squadrons of our group arrived that month, and our ground personnel landed at Port Said, bringing a convoy of American trucks and jeeps just in time to help two squadrons of us move to another field a few miles north of Haifa, called "St. Jean".

With our men and trucks came American canned food! Oh day of smiles and revelry! Now that we had our own cooks and mess equipment, we could dispense with our mess kits and eat more royally. The Army may move on its stomach but the Air Corps flies on it. We had eggs or French toast for breakfast, and frequently there were excellent pancakes with syrup. Sometimes we had good peach or chocolate or pumpkin pies. The fresh meat was a problem because it all tasted and looked like dried camel meat, which it may have been. After we objected to having carrots as the only vegetable for two weeks straight, we dieted quite well and even started putting on some weight. The argument against carrots was that the vitamins were doing our eyesight so much good, we couldn't tell when the sun went down.

Since our organization was not large enough to call for a Quartermaster or commissary, our food came from the British commissary in Haifa. Our new clothes came from the British military store called NAAFI (Navy, Army, Air Force Institute). One was located at a British cadet school a mile west of us on the shore of the Mediterranean. The loose-fitting English jacket called a "bush-coat" made a big hit with all our men, because it was thin, cool cotton and could be worn as something a little more dressy than our khakis.

When we started combat flying, Major Sturgis said we would all have to learn together. There was no one to teach us. I think we learned most from Benghazi. It was one of the hottest targets our heavy bombers worked over in the desert. Twelve of our B-24's were to blow up two large freighters that had survived the gamut of bombs and torpedoes and were unloading tanks and other materiel for Rommel. We had been after them the day before as they crossed the Mediterranean, but after hours of formation flying and dwindling dangerously low on gas, we had still seen nothing but water. This time we were determined.

We had Swetland's alarm clock set for seven o'clock. We dressed, had breakfast, performed our toilets, filled canteens, picked up our flight clothes and automatics, and then piled on an old British truck for the mile ride to the briefing room on the field.

Briefing was at eight. There was not much to it, because the Benghazi trip was becoming as common as a milk run. First Major Sturgis told us what we were after, and then showed the course on a map. He told the pilots which ships they would fly and in what position. He told the bombardiers the manner of using both bombsight and the lead plane as references for a good bomb pattern. There was no intelligence information for us, so we went back to the truck and rode to the planes.

We left our base at 9:30 A.M. In fifteen minutes we were in a V of V's heading westward down the Mediterranean, which had lain abed late and was still stretching in long smooth swells. To fool the listening posts at Crete on our right, and Matruh, Tobruk, and Beghazi on our left, we headed toward distant Malta.

The British Intelligence knew as much about German positions as the Jerries themselves did.

The formation was excellent at first. Ed and I took turns flying our ship on the Major's wing as two and a half hours went by. We were about 200 feet above that famous Mediterranean blue, when a call came in over the interphone:

"Enemy ship at 10 o'clock!"

I passed it on over the command radio as the turret behind me swung its gun overhead. The formation coiled like a steel spring. Twin-motored Junkers came into view, arced casually across our path, evidently thinking we were friendly. And then the steel spring let go! The turret guns barked rapidly over my head shaking dust loose around us, and red tracers came from all directions at the stranger, like long accusing fingers. The Junkers suddenly dove and twisted away, but already one motor trailed black plumage.

Beyond Crete (we saw only a small island off the southern shore of it), we began to climb -- too fast for several of our planes. At about 13,000 feet our plane showed signs of having difficulty in staying at the Major's side. Number-two engine fuel pressure was weak and needed a new pump. Now the gauge showed only five pounds, and we could hear the engine detonate. I reached under Ed's hand on the throttles and eased the manifolds pressure back to 37 inches with number two throttle. The motor seemed less anxious to cut out then, yet it pulled. We needed every bit of pull we could get. The pressure went up to six and a quarter pounds.

At low climbing airspeed in the thinner air, the motor temperatures teased the red line at 250 degrees. I enriched the mixtures beyond normal, and the temperatures held a while, then it climbed over the red line. I looked at Ed. We had our oxygen masks on now and only lifted them to speak when necessary. It was dangerous to remove them except at long intervals, but it was difficult to speak distinctly over the interphone when the mask was on. Ed was busy making the three good motors give maximum pull without giving a cylinder to eternity. He tried to keep the plane somewhere above stalling speed, and to stay on the Major's wing. Ed was busy!

Number four was hot so I flicked the cowl flap switch. In a few minutes I had the cowl flaps open a bit, but they acted as a drag. Ed shook his head and swore into his mask. I closed the flaps slightly. (Our motors were heating because of the unusually steep climb to make our arrival over the target more of a surprise. We learned that such a climb was costly and climbed more slowly thereafter.)

The Major had stressed the objective: the plane was to do the job -- motors could be replaced. I visualized his piercing eyes and bristly away-from-home mustache. All motors approached the limit, and number four faltered first. The r.p.m.s fell off and came back, but the momentary unbalance of power made the ship pivot 15° in flight, and it gave us an uncomfortable feeling. In the daylight we did not feel as helpless as we would at night. Two motors wouldn't lift our gas and bomb load. They wouldn't even hold our altitude, but we could salvo the bombs and glide more than 300 miles over sea toward home -- probably making it safely. In the daylight you can see where you are and know better what your situation is. It's the British with their faithful, but slower Wellingtons who prefer the night

We were lagging well behind now -- a lone target for pursuit. Ed pushed all the throttles. Number-two's fuel pressure went below six pounds again, and the motor detonated, but came back. Number four faltered more frequently. It was time to make the left turn to run on Benghazi. We were at 20,000 feet and mushing through the air. We could go higher, but not at the Major's rate. Right then he started a big circle because others had been dropping behind too. We cut across the circle and closed up to 600 yards -- but that wasn't close enough, and Benghazi was dead ahead. No enemy fighters were reported yet, but they would be sitting up there waiting for stragglers. Our ship was operating at absolute maximum. Another inch of manifold pressure would scatter cylinders into the rarified air.

Ed and I were still warm enough with the heaters working and the intense sun glaring into our "greenhouse." Our dark glasses would fog up sometimes when warm air escaped from the masks, and the metal by the window was too cold to keep a hand on. The free-air gauge registered minus fourteen degrees Centigrade. An hour and a half ago sweat dripped from our arms. I knew the crew in the tail must be frozen at their guns, so I checked with them on the interphone, as much to relieve the suspense and be sure we were ready, as to assure them they weren't forgotten. The vociferously swearing tail-gunner started to extemporize his condition in the drafty turret, but remembered orders. I received a muffled okay from everyone. At 24,000 feet the formation leveled off, and we closed up and throttled back to cruising power. I became aware of a sound as though the propeller blades were hitting chunks of air in that rarified atmosphere. My imagination was on the loose. I checked instruments. All okay.

Our run on into land was good. The Major's navigator had done a fine job. The landfall was just east of Benghazi on the hump. The harbor far below appeared photographic black, and the long cement moles where the ships were anchored stood out easily. (On our chart, the moles were named "George" and "Harry.") It was a peaceful scene with scattered white clouds at about 3,000 feet. We kept as far offshore as we could to keep the end of our bomb run far from the ground ack-ack batteries.

I heard a rumble behind me, then a roar of air. The bomb bay doors had rolled open. I turned in my seat to check them. Now we swung on the speck that was our freighter.

"On course!" came over the interphone from the bombardier.

Ed answered, "Level!"

A stick of five bombs left the lead ship. I concentrated on our own bomb-release signal. It should flicker now -- no -- now! What in hell was the matter?

Just as the Major swung into a 90-degree turn, our ship jumped. The bombs were gone! The electric releases must have frozen, and now the bombardier had salvoed. Some spot of open water would be broiled up. I whipped a glance at Ed's face. That was all I needed: I wondered how much it would take for a man to explode at 24,000 feet – and what a mess it would be for the co-pilot to work through! I was too mad to talk, but Ed was trying, and the words that spouted from his red face into the green oxygen mask fairly blew the mask off his face. The garbled mess the throat microphone allowed to boil into the interphone must have thawed out those rear gunners! Now the two right motors dropped earthward in a wingover as we held our place in formation. We twisted and dived for three thousand feet to avoid the black puffs now spouting around us. We shallowed our descent and started on our route home.

As we turned again, I could see smoke coming from the freighter, and there had been other hits on the mole. Now there was a trail of smoke and an occasional flame from up the mole beyond our target-- – we had hit either an oil dump or a small tanker. Ed and I exchanged glances again. His eyes wrinkled at the corners, and I knew he was grinning. So was I.

We had taken Benghazi by surprise –- but as I looked, the sky around the last element was black with ack-ack bursts. The anti-aircraft was really awake! I learned later that the last element of the formation had picked up enough flak for the whole squadron. It's interesting to watch the stuff hunt you out. First black puffs appear below or above you. Then they find your altitude and close in. If you're still on a straight course, the harmless-looking smoke rings get closer. Suddenly part of your windshield goes past your ear, or a motor lets off a trail of black smoke. The Germans sometimes anticipated our path and prepared a box of black bursts for us to penetrate. Aside from actual damage, the sight alone bothered the bombardiers.

There came a blur over the interphone – our tail gunner reported two pursuits climbing up below us. We looked around and down, but the pilots can never see anything from that little greenhouse. The rear gunners know twice as much about the result of a mission as the pilots. Suddenly, I noticed number four oil pressure was down to forty pounds, and it crept lower. Our waist gunner had reported "smoke" from number four, so we knew we'd been losing oil, but didn't realize so much was gone. We wanted to keep all the motors until we broke up formation at dark. Just then Ed shoved the throttle ahead a bit. He'd gotten word over the inter-plane radio that the pursuits were diving out of the sun, and at the same time I felt the ship jar as Taylor in the rear turret went into action. I knew all the rear guns were at work.

When your men start shooting, you tense up a bit and try to spot the fighter so you can tell how to maneuver. He comes streaming into your vision making you think your flaps are down or you're parked. Then he skitters high ahead and wings over to come back with red spots flashing where his guns are so that his ship seems to be afire. When he comes in from ahead, the bomber pilot tightens up more than ever until he becomes hardened to the sight.

The top turret was swinging to the left of the ship and I saw tracers leaving the other ships of our element.

"Into a spin" and "parachute," is what I could picked out on the interphone.

The pursuits (one Me 109 and one Macchi 200) had dived out of the low sun in between the wing ships to be safe from cross fire, because the waist gunners couldn't fire toward each other. But the tail turrets blasted when they were above and the side guns let go as they passed under. The Macchi that attacked us whipped into a spin, caught fire, and dived while the pilots bailed out. He had strafed one ship with little damage. The Me 109 had torn up one of the ships behind us a bit and shattered the knee of one of its waist gunners, but that enemy was diving in flames too.

A few minutes later a report of the injury came over the radio. They had administered sulfanilamide and a half-grain of morphine and were applying a tourniquet, but the boy was cold and would the formation go to a lower altitude to lessen chances of shock? We did, and by now the sun was about down, so we dropped into the desert haze that helped cut the light. The Major finally signaled to "break it up," and when we were spread out, we cut number four and feathered it.

I looked at the three blades standing straight into the wind, and contemplated the ingenuity of man. A blue flame from inside number three cowling stopped the reverie. It spat regularly, rapidly and outward from a cylinder, hitting against the cowling, where a white disk was appearing in the metal. Now I knew what had caused my "chopping chunks of air" sound -- one spark plug had blown out. The ignition from the other plug was shooting out a torch-like flame seen in the growing darkness. I pointed it out to Ed.

"Well, hell!" he said, "We've still got one good "fan" left!" and grinned to give me confidence. He continued balancing the ship's controls to offset the unequal pull of the three motors. Together we set the automatic pilot. As a safety precaution, I turned the fire extinguisher on number-three engine so that I only needed to pull the handle if the engine caught fire.

It was well past dinnertime -- eight o'clock -- and not much for us to do but peer into the darkness below and the star laden sky above and watch instruments. Occasionally white streaks would shoot near us out of the sky. The first one always startled us a bit, but then we knew they were just shooting stars. Sometimes they would burn out way below us.

I called Swetland and asked for his can opener. He passed it up, and I opened a can of grapefruit. The can was still chilled from altitude as though it had come out of the refrigerator. One of the best watermelons I ever had was one that a gunner brought aboard and handed out on the way home -- it was chilled through and through. Chadwick came out of his turret a minute to eat, and passed out some crackers and beef sausages.

This night flight home is almost the hardest part of the trip. The strain is over. There's little chance of fighter attack. Yet if you eat, sleep is as persistent an enemy as the Jerry. You check your course with the navigator, listen to the synchronous roar of the engines, and check instruments again -- oil and cylinder-head temperature, fuel and oil pressure, r.p.m.'s, the compass, and the altitude -- and that steady, uncompromising drone in your ears wants to put you to sleep. But you don't dare sleep. So you smoke and slouch down in your seat, or peer out for clouds or lights. Sometimes you can get a program on the radio in English from a commercial station in Cairo or Jerusalem. You pull back the window by your ear to flip the cigarette out and sniff fresh air. The sound is like the thunder of falling water at Niagara. It's just wind, but it's terrific. I remember teachers trying to convince me that air was substance. At air speed, it's a solid!

I checked instruments again. Number one oil pressure was fluctuating, but the trouble was probably the instrument. We had another two hours to go, but they passed safely. The Pleiades looked like weaving searchlights in the distance, until we finally identified them as the constellation on the horizon. I remembered another night the bulging redness of the rising moon looked like a burning ship.

As we approached the coast, the searchlights of Haifa were switched on for a landmark, and then they swung toward our field to help us locate it. We sighted the runway lights, identified ourselves, circled, and landed. Ed did a nice job on three motors

When the engine gasped to silence, Sgt. Weeks and his ground crew gathered around to hear about the trip and find out how their "baby" had behaved. This time we had quite a list of troubles for them.

A truck rumbled us to operations where two crews we already being interrogated. We got some hot coffee and reported what we knew of the mission. The tail gunner in the last ship had the most complete picture. He sees it all. We had hit Benghazi by surprise, set fire to two ships, damaged a third and dock installations, and shot down two fighters. It hadn't been the harrowing experience heavy bombers get occasionally, but with a little success and a little trouble we called it an average mission. A day later there was a report in the "Palestine Post" and probably in the papers at home: "Allied bombers again attack shipping and harbor installations at Benghazi."

Although we flew a variety of other missions, Benghazi always caused the most trouble and worry. Two of the ships we lost the first month had only been damaged over Benghazi. Most of the crew bailed out of one when they were as near home as Burg El Arab, but four men were with the plane when it crashed. The other hit a gas truck in a blackout landing on a desert landing ground. The only casualty was a cocker spaniel mascot.

Major Sturgis led a formation over Benghazi one day and, furious when the bombs didn't release, he turned the lead over to another ship and went over the target alone -- again. No sooner were the bombs away than he was jumped by a Messerschmidt 110 -- a powerful and deadly pursuit for one slow bomber to fight off alone. As the gunners fired their guns, they one-by-one found that every gun on the ship was jammed. There was no time to take the guns apart for repair, so with clever precision and a pair of powerful arms, if not with the utter coolness that a fictional character might have, the Major proceeded to out-maneuver the enemy pursuit until it expended all its ammunition. He dove for the protection of the desert until the enemy was boring in for an attack, and then he pulled the giant ship around until it faced the pursuit and it had to break away to avoid collision after firing only a few bursts. The bomber twisted and dived and turned, always headed downward toward the desert at its maximum air speed.

To maneuver at such a speed took the strength of both pilots and should have torn the tail assembly off the ship, but somehow it didn't. The attack continued for half and hour, but before the bomber even reached the face of the desert, the enemy was out of ammunition and had to turn back. Major Sturgis landed in Egypt with his plane riddled with holes, but no one was hurt.

During an intensification of our raids on Rommel's supplies, Air Marshal Tedder came to our Field in the company of General Brereton. The DC-3 transport that was the General's plane pulled up near the operations building, and just as Tedder's feet touched the ground, there were two tremendous blasts half a mile down the taxi strip.

"The British are pretty much on the ball saluting their chief," I thought, not knowing whether or not they shot off guns in salute for an Air Marshal. But the blasts had not been intended. Two armament men had unloaded a pair of depth charges from a Blenheim, and forgetting to take out the fuses, rolled them down the taxiway toward the supply area. The explosion had disintegrated the two men and wounded five others.

Two of our men received Silver Star awards for their part in saving the life of a gunner. The formation had just left the target at an altitude of 23,000 feet when one of the waist gunners called the pilot to say that the gunner had passed out. There was no enemy near, so the pilot peeled from the formation and dove to a lower altitude. In the meantime, the navigator, using a walk-around oxygen bottle, hurried to the back of the plane. He ripped off the gunner's mask, which had frozen, and proceeded to take oxygen from his own mouth and exhale it into the gunner's mouth. In a few minutes the prostrate crewman showed signs of life, and the navigator gave him his own mask. The old style masks had a restriction where exhale moisture could condense and freeze. It almost never happens in modern masks.

Most of our fatalities were among waist gunners, because they were least protected from bursting ack-ack. Vests were later devised that put an armored layer over their bodies. The fact that our men had their bodies gored by shell fragments doubtless saved the lives of later gunners, but it was hard to focus on a cosmic picture when your squadron's blood and flesh was spattered on the planes. No one on our own crew had as yet been injured.

The war correspondents in Cairo were finally allowed to accompany us on a long mission, and it turned out to be the one to Navario Bay. Some excellent accounts written by Lake of INS and Kennedy of AP appeared in the home papers, and Winston Burdett broadcast his account from Cairo. Their men who had been in a British retreat in Greece and Crete saw more of a symbol in this mission than did the men who flew the planes. To the correspondents, it meant something to be on the "giving" end of an air raid, and to be coming back to the scene of defeat at Greece. For that reason, the Navarino raid was given greater acclaim than we thought it deserved.

There were two tankers anchored in the harbor, one of which we splashed water on. We may have damaged it under the water line. Part of the defenses there, in addition to the ack-ack batteries in the hills, were the guns of two cruisers anchored inside submarine nets at the outer edge of the bay. After the bombing, the German radio that controlled the fighters proved to be on the same frequency that we were using, and by talking back and forth between our planes, we managed to interrupt the messages the German controller was trying to send. But the Germans would interfere with our messages, too. Someone was seriously wounded in one of our planes, and the Major couldn't make out all of the pilot's messages, so he finally shouted: "Get the hell off the air!" In the pause that followed, he received the message.

That night as we flew home, the long-expected windshift of the season took place, and the wind blew from the southeast instead of the west. Some of the navigators were not aware of the change, and two ships were blown north of their course. One of the pilots who landed an hour and a half late told of seeing some black clouds vaguely discernable against the horizon. He disliked clouds and gained altitude to avoid them. Those "clouds" were the mountains that rise straight up from the water at Beyruit, Syria. The other plane missed the first line of peaks and crashed into the second.

The British believed that their surprise raid on Tobruk of about September 13 was tipped off, because the Allies took quite a beating that night. The British lost several destroyers and a cruiser, the landing parties were subjected to heavy cross-fire from machine guns, and approximately eight out of twelve B-25's were lost. Our planes were at 8,000 feet while the '25's were about 4,000. One of our pilots reported feeling his plane jolt from an explosion below him, and he saw something black hurtle upward past his cockpit. We now believe it was part of a B-25 that exploded in mid-air 4,000 feet below him.

The greatest number of our missions went against enemy ships as they crossed the Mediterranean. Rarely was a destroyer risked to guard them. Usually they were sent alone many miles apart. The precision with which the British gave us the future position of these ships was astounding. Although we had to search over a given area, there was a minimum of error involved, and seventy-five percent of the time we found our target. We usually came down to twelve or sixteen thousand to bomb just out of range of the ship's guns where we could take our time and bomb accurately.

When Rommel's fuel situation was even beyond the point of merely being critical, two tankers were reported to us as having a probable destroyer escort. I think every B-24 that the Americans and British had was out that day. Our flight spotted one tanker through the haze after two other formations had passed over it. There was no destroyer within sight, so we took our time to make a good approach and bomb run. We didn't know that the Crete listening posts had picked us up and that ten Me. 110's were on their way out. The bomb hits on the doomed ship were barely reported when Taylor frantically called in that a big flight of enemy planes was behind us. For thirty minutes there was a battle royal. The enemy at first tried to stay out of our range and above us, lobbing in their cannon shells, but when that brought no results, they bored for a kill. We saw two pursuits hit the sea. The rest broke off the fight earlier than we had expected, probably because the ship they were sent to protect was already in flames. Our planes had only a few holes and no one was injured.

Usually when we returned from a mission, the searchlights at Haifa went on to give us a landmark, because they were able to tell at quite a distance whether we were friend or foe. They were low-level lights used for low-flying planes and for lighting the waters of Haifa harbor in case a submarine tried to creep in a night.

On returning from the engagement with the 110's, we missed the helter-skelter swinging of the Haifa lights which looked for all the world like two teams of baseball players swinging white bats over their heads for their warm-up. We found that we were over land without seeing a light of any kind, nor could we find any familiar sight. We had no idea whether the lights were extinguished because of enemy planes, or whether we were off our course. Our gas was getting dangerously low, and one engine was feathered because an oil line had broken. Just as we were debating on whether to bail out or try a night crash landing, we saw a dull red blinking light below us. When we shot off a double red distress flare, a green flare answered from the ground a few seconds later. In the English system, a dim single line of lights or flare pots was used on the left side of the runway, the pilot's side of the ship, and from that we could tell, without having radio communication with the ground, that we were to land west. We had no idea what field it was, since the code letters blinked by the red light were not listed on our radio "flimsy," as the information sheet was called.

Ed was physically and nervously worn as he brought the ship down to earth. We had been in the air for twelve hours. We both strained our eyes into the darkness to be sure of accurately judging our height and the position of the lights. It's best not to rely too much on an altimeter at low altitudes, especially if it was last adjusted to atmospheric pressure twelve hours before. When we were close enough, I switched on a landing light so we could see the mottled surface of the camouflaged runway more easily. We were too close for the power we were pulling. We had a little extra power for safety. Now Ed cut the engines back abruptly and nosed the ship down close to the runway. He pulled his control back slowly, waiting for the plane to settle down -- but it didn't settle. The patches of runway and the flickering flare-pots slipped past, and still we floated. The weight of the ship was much less that he had anticipated, since the weight of gasoline was almost gone, so we were still flying when ordinarily we would have been on the ground. With one engine out, there was only one approach for landing. To put power on again could be disastrous.

We both leaned forward in our seats trying to see how long the runway was and what was at the end -- whether rock pile or open field. At last there came the vibration of touching the ground. We both put our feet on the brakes and waited as the ship lost speed and the end of the runway loomed closer – with an open field beyond. He bumped off into about 300 feet of the field and turned around, waiting for instructions to taxi on this strange field. We waited and nothing happened for fully ten minutes, so we taxied out of the direct line of the runway and cut the engines. As we crawled stiffly out of the ship, glad to stretch our sore hips and backs after twelve hours of sitting, we heard the drone of four planes overhead and saw their green and red running lights

"Looks like they're circling to land," Swetland said.

"Those lights look almost far enough apart to be B-24's," Ed observed.

My only thought was that I wished some one would show up to put some food in me and tuck me in bed -- even the Sergeant Major-- thinking of the British song, "Sergeant Major, Be a Mother to Me". It had been a long time since we had finished that can of grapefruit and the sardines.

Just then the dim headlights of a wildly bouncing car came across the field and a tall British officer with a tremendously bushy mustache, all out of proportion to his face, jumped out.

"For God's sake, get that plane out of here! We've a whole flight that wants to land -- they're just about out of gas!"

He was the "Duty Pilot" in charge of the airdrome. I had seen him at Fayid just a week or so before. We tried to convince him that we were out of the way, but he would take no chance, and we finally had to start the engines and taxi about 300 feet farther.

The planes were given the green flare. And as they came in to land, we saw that they were Liberators -- the early B-24's that were made for the British.

When we were all together at the Officers' Club after interrogation, we found that these fellows had been the first flight out after the convoy. They had missed it, but reported seeing a ship in flames on the way back, which confirmed the success of our bombing.

This field, which was near Tel-Aviv, was Akier. With the threat of a possible Nazi push past El Alamein line to the Suez, the squadron had been moved back to Palestine. There are no better hosts in the world, I'm sure, than the British. Their officers' messes and their bars are always up to snuff, no matter what the facilities in general might be, and the ground officers, who were not worn out from the flight, hurried around to find beds for us on their crowded and unsettled post. They had a few permanent buildings of stone. In one of these over-filled places, Thompson and Swetalnd were given beds, and Gimble and I drew mattresses on the floor. I soon found out I was not alone in my bed, and spent a good deal of the night scratching, but when morning came, I was awakened by the sound of a black boy putting a hot cup of good English tea on the floor beside me, and the discomforts of the night were quickly forgotten

That morning, while the English mechanics fixed the broken oil line, our whole crew sat in the shade of the wing and played blackjack. For once, Ed had a hard time being the winner, because Chadwick, the radio operator, was pretty sharp at keeping the deal and managed to end up with most of our change.

We took off before noon, and on arriving at St. Jean found that they had received Ed's arrival message from Akier all right, but there had been a catastrophe the night before.

Our own field had been dark when the other ships landed. Major Sturgis was afraid that enemy planes would follow us home some time and strafe or bomb us in the light of our fields. For that reason the runway lights were so dim they could scarcely be seen, and the Major always landed without wing tip running lights.

One plane had landed and was being guided to its revetment by ground crews with their flashlights. At one point the taxi strip came within seventy-five feet of the runway. It was here that the plane faced the runway and paused for a moment. The pilot retarded his engines while the engineer, a kid named Woods, stood in the top hatch to check their progress. When the engines turn too slowly, the generators cut out, but the batteries should continue the operation of the electrical equipment -- including the wingtip lights. But the lights went out. Over the sound of their own motors, no one heard the unlighted plane that was descending to land. The approaching plane had drifted a bit to one side of the runway, but a slight kick on the rudders would bring it back in time to land on the pavement.

Ted, the co-pilot of the ship was on the ground, saw it first -- an engine on a wing of blackness. He ducked and pulled the pilot down below the windows with him. The wing came through the propellers of Ted's plane like a ham in a slicer. Clip--- clip -- clip and the approaching wing was in sections. It all happened in a second. There was a quick, harsh scrape as the wing tip glanced off the top turret. The pilots were sick. They didn't have to turn around to know that Woods was gone. The wing had struck so hard that his shoes dropped into the plane. His twisted body was 100 feet away.

From the bomb bay came a frightened question from the engineer's inseparable friend, "Where's Bill? Where's Bill?" Then he saw the shoes and knew.

Bill had been a youngster who had lied about his age to join the Air Corps, but had been so fine an engineer that he was going to be made ground crew chief.

It was a drunk night at the post, and a somber one. By the fault of no one, a fine boy and a greatly liked engineer, was suddenly and horribly dead. Particularly for the other men of that crew, there was no answer, so they got drunk. Woods was buried in a Haifa cemetery the second day.

One of the most successful raids was carried out by a squadron that had proceeded us to Palestine. On one of their

Benghazi raids they scored a direct hit on an ammunition ship that was tied up at one of the moles sticking out into the harbor. The blast and destruction were terrific! From 20,000 feet they could see the tremendous white flash. The ship was annihilated, and a complete section was blown out of the concrete mole. Flying debris and the underwater concussion itself likely damaged other ships nearby. When Benghazi was finally captured, its harbor was an area of completely wrecked ships and moles from this and other raids.

But not all our Benghazi missions were good. For a long time a cloud mass that was 200 or more miles in diameter rose from its terrific rain and squalls at ground level to a towering, icy height of 30,000 feet. We called it a stationary front. At any time it might move slightly and leave our target open for bombing. Time after time we flew from Palestine to Benghazi -- an eleven or twelve hour mission -- to see if we could bomb. There was no way of getting the information in advance. We would usually take the land route, flying low over Egypt with its network of rivers and irrigation canals and green land. We would see ancient brown buildings and temples, men and women working tediously by hand or with an ox and a wooden plow. They would look up as the formation droned on overhead, and flocks of frightened white cranes would rise and wing to another field. Then, abruptly, we were over the desert and within sight of the endless convoy of trucks that flowed like a conveyer belt along the road between El Alamein and Egypt. The traffic was not confined to the road, and for a mile on either side were the tracks of tanks and armored cars and other vehicles. As we flew on, the sand showed white salt lines, and damp-looking areas grew larger.

This was the quicksand of the Qattara Depression that held Montgomery's southern flank. There would be an occasional jeep or tank track winding along the narrow strips of higher ground. On the north and west sides of the depression were rugged 100-foot walls of jagged rock that led up to that level of the desert. When we saw the wall curving toward us from the north, we would gain a little altitude to clear the western rim. There were one or two places in the west wall that had steep gulleys where a powerful vehicle could climb and the tracks of the depression floor led these. On out across the desert there was little to see but the dull pink sand and rock that our planes were colored to blend in with. Never was there a person or a car in sight because during the intense heat of the day nothing moved from its shade unless forced out. Farther on, as we were beginning to gain altitude, we passed over the broad barbed wire fence of the Italians that stretched south past the holy Giarabub Oasis of the Senoussi. Here the Italians maintained a fort and an ack-ack battery.

Then came the tedious climb to altitude, reaching 20,000 feet as we approached the edges of the front. There were holes in the clouds at first, and we twisted through them. Sometimes we would suddenly be enveloped in clouds. We then spread out to avoid hitting each other while we flew by instruments. The wings and windshield and propellers would ice up, and usually the planes became too scattered to proceed to the target safely even if they finally came out in the clear again. Then we would have to turn for the long, but happy trip home alone -- happy, because we were not to be shot at that day. It was a relief to have to turn back finally, but before that moment, there was a self-battle for the pilot, who must decide when conditions were so bad that he must turn back, He wanted to make that turn long before, but fought off the feeling--fought off those little fears and doubts that escaped from the unconscious mind and bounced into his thoughts in a spirit of self-preservation. These had to be sorted out and confined to make room for a logical listing of factual pros and cons. The engine temperatures climbed to a maximum, and the controls became sloppier as the air grew thinner -- they also lost their tension as the cold contracted the fuselage of the plane more than it did the control cables. Perhaps the worst source of physical and mental discomfort was the oxygen mask. It closeted the face and kept it moist, if not dripping. It bound at the nose where it had to fit tightly, and it easily blew loose at the chin. If it didn't fit right, every breath blew steam over the dark glasses. And if the heaters of the plane didn't work, the pilots, who didn't have electric suits and gloves, had trouble keeping their hands warm in any glove they could grip the wheel with. Slowly they were losing instantaneous control of their planes as they approached the enemy. Knowing this and anticipating the enemy action was enough to breed "combat colic" -- a man did not need a physical wound. It is little wonder that men have over-estimated the danger to their ships and themselves and turned back. We even had a case of two men who turned in their wings rather than fly out again after they had seen gaping holes torn in their planes and the adjacent ones; had seen ships spiral earthward out of control carrying their friends to death; and had seen other friends near death when the flight reached home.

On the other hand, many men are able to laugh at their own fears. A poem written by Lt. William Robinson, a bombardier in our squadron, had a wide circulation. It laughed at what we all considered an ideal -- to be through with combat. But it doesn't tell of the human reaction toward those who achieved release from combat and were promoted to a "softer" job behind a desk -- the reaction of real bitterness.

THE RAVING

Once upon a mission dreary, when
of combat I'd grown weary,
I had flown a thousand hours and
was sure to fly some more,
Suddenly there came a knocking, sounding
like some ack-ack popping--
Popping like the very devil just beneath my bomb bay door.
"Tis some Jerry," thought I, "Who is
wishing to improve his score.
I will use evasive tactics, even if he does get sore."

Turning then, I saw before me, blacker now than e'er before,
Ack-ack bursting close and heavy;
guess I better turn some more.
Open wide I rolled the bomb doors,
and to my surprise and horror
Flashing fast and bright below me were
some ninety guns or more.
I remembered then the briefing when
they told us with much speaking,
There would be but three or four

Leveling then, I made a bomb run,
which was not a very long one,
For the Varsity was on duty, and I'd seen their work before.
Then an engine coughed and clattered,
and the flank around me splattered

And I knew they had my number, just
my number, nothing more.
Then at last the bombs were toggled
and, alone, away I hobbled
With some fifty-seven inches and a feathered number four,
While outside, like ducks migrating,
was a drove of Me.'s waiting --
Waiting all with itching fingers set to even up the score.

I had lost my upper turret, and alone, defenseless, worried
I was then the scariest bastard mortal woman ever bore,
For each bright and screaming tracer
coming nearer, ever nearer,
Made my spirits sink within me, just
my spirits, nothing more.

Then at last, to my elation, I caught up with my formation,
And the Me.'s turned and left me, by
the tens and by the scores;
But my wings were torn and shattered,
and my nerves completely tattered,
And as you can plainly see, at least for me, the war is o'er.

Now my sinuses start seeping every
time they mention briefing,

And for this distressing symptom I will rate my double bars;
And I'll have my fun and frolic and a case of combat colic
      Here in Cairo with the Cossacks, 'mongst
          the "eagles" and the"stars".

Now I've learned the art of living, and my secret I am giving
      To the rest of those among you who
         might care to live some more,
      For my sinus (whisper "briefing")
      Still is seeping, still is seeping.
      No more flying, no more missions,
        no more combat, nevermore.

Sometimes when we were in the vicinity of this cloud mass over Benghazi, we would create real beauty. In that cold, clear air nearly saturated with water vapor, the additional moisture from the exhaust of our motors formed long white veils of ice clouds which marked our path of flight. Over a target such trails would be a dangerous give-away to a surprise raid or assist accurate prediction for ack-ack fire. It was awe-inspiring to fly through the magnificent white valleys of the cloud tops but, time after time, weather was our enemy, no matter how beautiful a gown she wore.

On the way home we would sometimes pick up German propaganda programs on the radio. Two men would laugh and joke in not-too-good English, and once they talked about the Roosevelts as Jews -- a cripple and a proprietress of a French Catholic brothel. We were not sure of all the significance they intended, but after dropping fifty tons of bombs on German targets, we felt we could laugh, too -- for the joke was on them.

Chapter III

ON ALERT

Superstition plays a subtle hand. If anyone were to ask the men of our squadron, perhaps half would admit they were superstitious. Out of the fifty flying officers, perhaps two were entirely without recourse to a symbol of extra-human assistance.

If someone had asked me "Are you superstitious?" I would have answered "Hell no!" I'd have thought no more of it, and continued being careful to wear my "dogtags" on every mission. Because it was regulation? No. Because if I was prepared for recognition after death, death would never come.

Jerry was more obvious, because he carried a rabbit's foot on his key chain. Once Jerry kiddingly remarked, as we buckled on our gun belts before hopping the truck down to briefing, "After that poker session last night, the Good Lord is really on my side. I owe so much money everybody's gonna pray for me till I get back on the ground!" He wasn't serious, though.

And eventually I uncovered Ed's superstitions. During a flight, we record on a form our names, where we go, how long we fly, and other pertinent data. In the form there is also a box where the number of landings is recorded. Ed never allowed that square to be filled in until we were on the ground. It was unlucky.

Sometimes our missions flew every other day -- sometimes only once a week. Between missions we were "on alert", but the picture we presented was more like Miami Beach at the height of the tourist season. Our buildings at St. Jean were of brick with tin roofs that metallically amplified the sound of the rain. In each building were five rooms opening onto a shaded verandah, and each room housed the four officers of a crew. It was a mental effort to struggle out of our netting and soft beds in time for breakfast if there was nothing to do that day. Although we dressed to go across the road to breakfast, we peeled again to a pair of shorts and shoes when we retuned to the shade of the porch.

When we went to town, we picked up an occasional good book and soon we had a circulating library with "I have dibs on that next" as the only library card. A great portion of time was spent reading, re-reading, and writing letters, and we would sit and talk about home or rumors or experiences or plans or people. One of the rumors that started after we'd been there about two months had the first pilots going home to instruct and the co-pilots taking over. We started checking out the co-pilots officially, but the rumor changed to sending the pilots home after 300 combat hours, and we cooled off. The highest man had about 130 hours. The importance of our job meant little to us because of our impersonal relation to the enemy. If we had known we would be in combat for another full year, our immediate depression would have been unlimited. Another rumor had us going to the Russian front, but that too withered away.

Some of the boys would spend hours working on their fingernails. Someone with ambition might get up and put on a pair of pants to go down to the gate and get a chocolate bar from a little stand just outside. The Palestine chocolate was good, but it didn't last long in the hot weather. A few of the boys kept picture albums and spent time on those, having the films developed and printed at a little Jewish shop in Nahariah where we went swimming.

In the time that the four of us had been together, the very nature of our jobs had paired us off -- the pilots as against the two who shared the nose of the plane together. Bus seats and sleeping facilities seemed to come in twos, and those things tended to make us pair off in other pursuits.

Thompson was a strange personality to me in many ways. He was quiet and reserved. Although he was in charge of the plane and crew, we shared opinions quite freely on all matters, and he often took my suggestion if he thought it better. And yet, there was a thread of a strain between us that I couldn't place for a while. I first put my finger on it when I found him building up a section of his stamp collection from a little store in Haifa that I hadn't run across. He seemed to have always overlooked mentioning it, but he knew I was collecting stamps too -- we had bought some together. And there were other signs that he was trying to outdo me for some reason.

I looked up to Ed as someone ahead of me in age and flying time. In addition to that, he had proved to have a cooler head and sounder judgment than his quietness and unimpressive appearance indicated. He had become one of the three flight leaders of the squadron.

On one of the last days of August, the 29th I think, he rolled out of bed without the ability to quite cover up a smile of almost childish self-satisfaction, which once in a while tightened his lower lip and the corners of his mouth. By noon, I could take it no longer

"O.k., Bub," I said, hoping to surprise the truth out of him. "What's the big secret? And get that damn silly grin off your face!"

His eyes brightened into a full-fledged laugh before his face broke into a big grin. With a gesture of his arms like a bashful little girl throwing chicken feed from an apron, he gloated, "It's m'birrrthday!"

"Well, for Pete's sake! Happy birthday!" I said with more enthusiasm than originality, and extended my hand in congratulation. "And how many eons does that make you?"

"Hell," he said, "I'm twenty-two."

"You're what?" I asked in amazement, but as I asked I knew he wasn't kidding

"I'm still in m'prime," and he turned away, grinning at the surprise punch he'd pulled. Some of the other men in their rooms had heard our conversation and poked their heads out to see if Ed had been kidding. Everyone in camp was as surprised as I. We had been so sure of his age and wisdom.

Ed and I finally committed ourselves to developing a mustache. Only those who have tried can appreciate the suffering, the patience, and the care of such an enterprise. His was trim and mine was bushy. After one fretful month we were again clean-shaven. Swetland and Gimble attempted mustaches too. Theirs were less of an accomplishment than ours.

Swetland -- Paul -- had a queer little trick of giving an embarrassed, almost apologetic grin or laugh when he spoke, and if someone didn't know him, he might get the idea that Paul was easy to get around. But that just wasn't the case. He very pleasantly went his own sweet way. Like the time he bought a flute and a clarinet and an ocarina. The three of us had to live in the same cubicle with the noise he made, so no one complained louder than we did. Paul would sit for hours on the edge of his cot, playing his clarinet mostly from memory. Either his memory or the instrument wasn't all it should have been. After he'd play a phrase of some popular song for half an hour while we tried to read the same page over an over or to write a coherent letter -- after he'd hit every combination of half-tone, wrong notes, and squawks we thought possible, we'd voice our complaints:

"Look, Old Man," Jerry would say, "You have there a very fine instrument. This music you are struggling with, and murdering, if I may be permitted to be quite frank, was written by an able composer, yet the sounds that are crumbling the plaster of our little room are positively unbearable, Why don't you take a hint and find yourself a good book?'

Paul would look up with the brightest of sympathetic expressions -- sympathy for our feeble mentalities, not for our suffering.

"You mean you don't like it, huh? I think I'm gettin' better all the time. All I need is a little practice. Or maybe you'd rather I'd play my ocarina?" He'd smile a bashful smile and go right on playing that clarinet. He was so sweet about the whole thing. Paul was just too friendly to get really sore at, so we "sweated him out" while he practiced on this music, and in time he furnished the accompaniment for our informal sings. Every time the mail came in, Paul would get a letter from his mother. They were long letters and he studied every word. She would slip packages of Dentyne gum into his letters, and frequently two batteries for his penlight would come in a little jewelry box. There would be cookies and candies and more things than I can remember. Paul's letters to his mother were long too. He told he every detail of what we were doing that he could tell. The planes that shuttled their messages back and forth helped to maintain the closest consideration between a mother and a son that I have ever known.

The more I knew Jerry, the more he resembled Wayne Morris, the movie star -- big and blond and carefree, He had an athletic step that was a joy to watch, but being an athlete didn't help hair grow on his upper lip. Jerry was a glad-hander and a socialite, but no politician -- he was to honest. To him, the world was a lot of fun. His zest for living was wonderful and contagious. It made no difference whether he was stretched out on his cot for an afternoon nap, or in a whirl of conversation at a bar, or even on a bomb run. He dozed most of the way to the target. At first the black puffs worried him to the extent that he made the bomb runs too short, but his faith in Lady Luck held out, and he grew to concentrate on the bombsight even when a piece of glass in the nose broke loose and cut his flying clothes. But he was no bombardier because he was not careful and exacting enough. Ed almost lost his position as a flight leader at one time due to his erratic bombing.

Sometimes Jerry's deep, soft voice would ascend to the treble clef as he awkwardly tied himself up in an explanation.

"What I mean is -- " and he pecked his face forward like a rooster after a single grain of corn. His big right hand tried to frame in the air whatever it was his mind could picture and his words could not.

Jerry brought home to the other three of us chronicles of gaiety and troubles in the Haifa nightspots. One such story illustrates the silly friction sometimes arose between the Americans and the English. One night -- it was one of the first that our fellows spent in town -- an officer with Gimble, his name was Fred, was packing his .45 automatic. There were four Americans and about a dozen Englishmen in a beer hall. When the Americans entered, the orchestra was interspersing its numbers with British marching songs. After the British national anthem was played, Fred and another officer yelled for the American national anthem. Some of the British were a little annoyed by the request, as their disgusted looks indicated. Beer descended and spirits rose. The Americans called for more American numbers and even booed when a British piece was played. The atmosphere tensed like the muscles of a jungle cat that smells blood. The Limies were noisy and boohed back, but the booh had a snarl in it. The Americans sat up straight in their chairs and braced their feet outside the legs -- clear of the table

Fred was from the open spaces of Oklahoma. When he was sober, there wasn't a shrewder, more just mind in the squadron. He was a flight leader above Thompson. But alcohol chopped into his veneer and intellect like a keen ax.

The level of his intelligence descended until hate and passion and stupidity lay raw on the surface.

Two Englishmen rose to their feet, stalked slowly toward the door, cinching up their belts. One of them, a burly animalistic fellow, motioned the Americans towards the door with a nod of his head. At this point Jerry was worried. He didn't like a brawl for its sake alone, and four of them were obviously outnumbered. Fred was savagely ready to take on everyone in the place, but he was in no hurry. He knew they would wait. It was within a few minutes of closing time -- twelve midnight -- and two more Englishmen left before the proprietor began to turn off the lights one by one. The music had stopped, and the scuffing of feet, banging of tables, and clinking of glasses was louder than the growl of men talking among themselves.

The four Americans shot to their feet, and kicked the chairs toward the table. They moved slowly and deliberately towards the door fifteen feet away. Three Tommies were behind them, and without warning they swung with their fists, catching Jerry on the shoulder blade and Fred behind the ear. The Americans immediately wheeled around with their fists flaying out -- at eight Englishmen. It was a sloppy melee of fists, but a square blow hit Fred on the cheek and bruised his eye. Like a bull with its head down swinging its horns, Fred cleared a space around him and made what could have been a fatal mistake. In his blind fury, he grabbed his .45 automatic from its holster and charged it. The men opposing him paused a split second in bewilderment, but before the gun could come to a firing position, a powerful blow from behind knocked it out of his hand. The four men from outside had come in to join the fight. The fight again went furious and blind, with a few solid blows landing on the Americans, and many fewer landing on the Limies. Suddenly the fighting stopped as though it were a breeze overcome by a tornado. Four British M.P.s broke up the fight, collared as many men as they could hold, and bundled them out the door to the police station two blocks away. Jerry and all but two of the Englishmen escaped out the door and disappeared into the darkness.

The next day, the other Americans, battered and bruised, showed up in camp. It was a week before Fred was able to get his gun from the police.

Most of the officers who went into Haifa to spend their time and money knew at least one girl they could count on for dates. She was "his girl". Major Sturgis had a few dates with a nice Russian, but Gimble showed up more frequently at the nightspot she frequented. Soon she was Gimble's girl. He used to tell us about the trouble he had with her Great Dane. Every time he made a pass at her, the dog proceeded to chew on him until the girl shooed the dog away. Jerry had no intention of giving her up, although he felt a little uncomfortable whenever he saw the Major. I don't think the Major really cared, but the thing built up in Gimble's mind like a cumulus cloud in the tropics. He brooded over it, and the brooding soured to hatred. Drinking loosens hatred into words that can't be retracted. Stirred by what he considered an injustice to a fellow bombardier, Gimble became well washed in his cups one night and boiled out hatred to the Major's face. The Major simply told him he was drunk and ordered him to his barracks. The problem in Gimble's mind were not dissipated by this encounter and so continued to grow.

Among us was an officer who, I suspect, was blessed with a trace of Indian blood. But when it comes to liquor, the trace of blood is no blessing. When he was drunk, he was wild. Sometimes he put on quite a show. I remember hearing Gimble describe the night he was dancing in the center of the floor with an ample-hipped woman. The music changed to a rumba, and, giving herself to the approved grace of rumba movement, she tossed her hips rhythmically from side to side. The officer stepped back and appraised his partner. With a bellow, he cried, "Lady, if you can do that in bed, you're worth a million bucks!" Gimble said the lady accepted the statement calmly. The other women within hearing discontinued their rumba.

Almost every day someone would rattle the dice, announce that the "Casino was now opening," and a crap game would gain momentum on the porch.

I'll never forget the day an English Tommy strayed up from his camp down near the airfield. There was one of the bigger games going on and perhaps twenty men, clad in their undershorts and shoes, were gathering around the players, so that little could be seen from outside except the hole in the middle whence came the babble of "crap" language.

"Four open .... Faded .... O.k., Dice, natural for me ... eighter for Decatur, the country set of Wise .... not hard, Dice, just big ....big six .. two notches, up, Dice ... that's it, come on, Pretty Dice ... it's crappin' time ... attention, Dice ... come on, apologize, Pretty Dice, apologize to Daddy ...."

The Limey reached the outside of the circle and tried to peer in. He didn't stand a chance. He went around to a thinner edge, but he still couldn't see. He leaned a little hard on someone, and the fellow, seeing it was an Englishman, opened up a trifle. Still the cries came out: "How many days in the week, Dice?" … "Four" … "Let's make that four, Dice" … "Fordyce, Arkansas, just a little town between Little Rock and Pine Bluff on the Arkansas River Pike."

The Limey bumped someone else, and smiled a little sheepishly.

"Bloody good, ain't it!"

Finally he worked himself to within view of the inner circle. In a slowly growing look of amazement, his jaw dropped to is lowest limit, and his eyes looked as though someone were pumping them up like balloons, as he saw the center floor carpeted with American and Palestinian money -- more than he would earn in years. Now that he could see what was going on, the enthusiasm of the game worked into his sporting blood, and gradually the pantomime motions of his head, urging the dice on, became vocal. Then he entered into the swing of the thing: "Cumawn, ya bloody dice. Rawl ot thot fo'r, no'!"

Little by little the Englishman's voice drowned out all others, and with a smile touching the corners of his mouth, Gimble handed the dice to the newcomer and covered his bet with a few coins. The circle expanded a little to give him room to work, as work he did. Those who couldn't keep their faces straight broke out of the ring and doubled up in convulsion of laughter in the yard. The Limey wound up like a cricket pincher and let go with a war cry: "All rought, ya bloody dice, crop fer me no'!"

The dice rattled against the pavement, and "crop" they did. The boys paid him off with pleasure, and gave him the dice again. It was more fun to watch him shoot than to win his small bets, and I think they changed the rules a bit to keep him in the game. When the game finally broke up for lunch, the visitor had a broad smile on his face as he hitched up his pants and tucked away his half a pound ($2.00) winnings.

"You Americans are sure a reckless lot," he said with a quirk in his head. He didn't know that he had earned the price of admission.

The little village of Nahariah, where we went swimming, was both a resort and a farm community. The citizens and shopkeepers were friendly to us, and their town offered more quiet pleasure for many of us than did the brighter nightspots of Haifa. The beach was broad and clean and the swimming was excellent. We would swim or doze or play ball, and anyone who happened to be flying would usually buzz low over the beach until we could see his face in the cockpit. We sometimes had to lie flat on the sand to duck the wings.

After swimming, we would go to one of several pensions or cafés for a good dinner and wine. A favorite was Gretel-Mayer's Pension just up the hill from the beach. While dinner was being cooked, we would sit on the verandah in comfortable summer chairs and sip the fine Carmel Hock wine. When the dinner of chicken or small steaks was ready, Mrs. Gretel-Mayer herself would usually summon us inside her lovely stucco house. She was a delightful bubbly-happy woman who dressed herself well, although she was quite heavy, and her hair curled in a short haircut. She couldn't manipulate the English language quite as well as her dapper husband, but she tried to learn our slang phrases. When we complimented her on her finely prepared meat or vegetables, she would effervesce happily and say: "I am cookink mit gaz, yes?"

There was a café up the street from Gretel-Mayer's called "Flatow". It was a vine-covered one-story building with a garden on one side that contained several groups of tables and a cement dance floor. I don't know who played in the orchestra at Flatow, but they played for the love of music. They swung out old German and Viennese pieces, and bits of classical works to a rhythm that made us sway and want to dance, but all we could do was watch the town's people enjoy it. Sometimes the musicians, as they left the orchestra corner to stroll around as they played, would stop and ask us to hum new American songs to them, and next time we came they were orchestrated. We spent some very lovely, though nostalgic, evenings in the dimly lighted garden at Flatow. Here was gaiety modulated by knowledge of war. War had brought something of peace to this village which had known heavy Arab attacks before this war. (The British captured two families of Nazis who had lived near Nahariah and had been inciting the Arabs against the town.(Many of Nahariah's men were serving at El Alamein.

Then at midnight the G.I. truck would rattle up to Flatow. We would climb aboard, and all the way home we sang "Jolly Sixpence" or "Bless 'Em All" or some of the old American standbys.

We were lucky to have had little disease in Palestine. A few boys caught malaria, but the exact number I don't know, because they were spirited away to a hospital so quickly we had little chance to see anyone really sick. General discomfort came from sandfly fever and dysentery. Sandfly rarely lasted more than twenty-four hours. It hit suddenly with eye ache, headache, fever, and chill, and then disappeared. Dysentery was a constant companion, despite the effort of the doctors to obtain adequate screening and food and garbage facilities. In the hot climate, food spoiled easily and the flies were everywhere. There was a mild form of dysentery called "the runs". It was disconcerting to be playing cribbage with wild enthusiasm, and to have your opponent suddenly cease his attention on the cards, and look through you with a blank stare. Politely avoiding a return stare, you notice he is taking mental soundings, just as surely as though he was heaving a lead line.

Suddenly he murmurs" Damn! Be back in a minute!" and without leaving his sitting position, he scurries off to the littlest building that stands all alone. That's why it's called "the runs". When there were twenty men darting in and out of the latrine all day long, the camp looked busy and "on alert".

Even the mildest of diseases hampered our missions, however. At high altitude over enemy territory facilities are embarrassingly inadequate. Crews simply had to be rearranged, and the healthy men had to fly time after time with no rest.

Any break in the skin festered quickly so that the smallest abrasion needed decisive attention promptly.

It was because of a quick-rising infection in my knee that I came to learn a bit about the English with which many Americans are not familiar. A great deal of reciprocal understanding will be important to our future peace, and I think one small comparison that was made might be worth repeating

I was in a hospital room with two British officers. One was a Captain with a dislocated shoulder, who was in charge of some Indian troops at El Alamein, and had been the manager of a tea plantation in Assam, India. The other, a 1st lieutenant, was an engineer who had come in from the desert east of the Suez Canal. He had been making preparations for the Army's possible occupation of that desert if Rommel broke through to Cairo, as they had been afraid he would.

Almost out of a clear sky, the engineer said, "Look here, your American cars aren't very good, are they!"

That slug left me dazed for a minute

"How do you mean that?" I asked.

"You people are always buying new cars -- you buy one every few years. Ours last fifteen or twenty years."

I had to think a minute to answer that one. I couldn't say our standards of living were different. It was unkind and it wasn't true. Our ideas were different and our cars had such farther to travel. We create cars in greater numbers than the British and by sales methods convince people they should change cars often. That makes work for more people and increases the flow of wealth. The British create a thing well, and they are proud of a product that lasts many years. Age and record mean a great deal to them, and by their standards we must seem shallow. Perhaps there are many trivial but conflicting ideas that will immeasurably retard understanding between the triumphant allies.

When I returned to camp there were eight letters for me. One was from the girl to whom I had been engaged. She just wanted to say hello, but that letter did something to me that hurt me deep inside as I had never been hurt by emotion before. In the letter was a small wisp of perfume that had been associated with the softness of her hair, the coolness of her ear, and the warmth of her lips -- with the satisfying tenderness of loving someone. I hurt inside as I never hurt before, and a poem came from my pencil:

SCENT IN A SOLDIER'S LETTER

I could see as well a moonbeam catch, as tell
That vague scent from half around the world.
Which rose, unmasked, and rushing to its task
Flooded a cooling. Hardening mind
With memories and passions now best forgotten.
A brief letter -- the words were naught:
She was well and working. Would I write?
But my heart was sickened when my scenes quickened
To a touch, a kiss, a smile of not too long ago
Awakened by this fleeting scent
From a world I'd nearly ceased to know.

In a place of death, disease and heat --
In ever-moving camps of men --
In sickening smells -- in foreign ways of life --
Their streets --

A fragrant, subtle, fading wisp of air
Had said in its own brief phase
All the words and thoughts of tenderness
Of which this life has long been purged.
And I ached inside; stricken by disease or lead?
No -- by a scent now gone,
For all the comfort, beauty, tenderness it urged
Must yet another while be dead.
I felt very sorry for one, William Gilbert

Chapter IV

TOURING THE HOLY LAND

The town of Haifa is not one of the old towns of Palestine. It lies on the north slope of Mount Carmel and is the Mediterranean seaport outlet for an oil line piped from Iraq. The population is one-half Jewish and is in the vicinity of 100,000. Jews from all over Europe have moved there as they have to Tel-Aviv

In the first week that we were in Palestine, Thompson, Swetland, Gimble, and I went into Haifa in the afternoon by means of British lorry that we happened to catch a ride on. After acquiring rooms at the comfortable Savoy Hotel, we proceeded to roam the streets. Since we didn't know just what we where getting into that first time, and the stories about fights between the Arabs and Jews were new to our ears, we each had a serviceable weapon of some kind along. Stuck under my belt and covered by my shirt was the slender knife I had purchased in Natal. We weren't looking for trouble, but we would be prepared for it.

The broad street a block or so removed from the waterfront is known as "The King's Way". The Palestine railway station is here, as are some of the larger furniture and dry goods stores. At the eastern end of the street toward the Arab section- are sheep pens and open street markets for fish, vegetables, and fruits where dirty, bearded venders cry their wares and black-robed Arab women with great loads of family goods on their heads stop to haggle over a cloth full of fish spread out at the edge of the street for display. Inside the open-fronted coffee shops, bearded men smoke and talk in groups, or play at a game similar to chess. The taxi companies are here and their sharp-eyed drivers are very alert for business. The ordinary cars, the latest of which are 1939 and 1940 Chevrolets, Pontiacs, Fords, or European cars, make the short local runs, and long sleek comfortable seven-or-more passenger touring cars make the longer runs to Tel-Aviv, Jerusalem, or Beyruit.

To the west, King's Way goes through the lowest part of the residential district out to the beaches and around Mount Carmel. On the streets that wind up the hill form King's Way are the many small shops that have anything you want to buy, and many more things you don't. The particular item of the gift shops that interested us was the fine silver filigree work. There are also wooden inlaid boxes, and brocades in bolts or made into jackets or coats. The merchants insist they have only one price when you start to bargain with them, but if you hold out long enough, they may make a special concession just for you. There are sports shops and candy shops and ice cream parlors, whose dishes are hard hit by the war restrictions.

As it grew dark, we went to our hotel for a fine four or five course meal worth the trip to town. Stepping beyond the heavy curtain at the hotel door, the darkness of the street was a surprise we hadn't anticipated. For the first time we knew how black a city could be in a war time. When our eyes became accustomed enough to the dark so that we could make out the outline of people passing by, we proceeded down the street toward a place we had noticed during the day. In the narrow streets we continually rubbed shoulders with ragged, sinister looking Arabs padding along through the filthy streets in their bare feet. All around were the sounds of people who couldn't be seen. An occasional store window that was painted blue let out enough of a glow to show that it was open for business, and it was into one of these that we went first in search of a drink and some music. The tavern consisted of a pair of dimly lit rooms with perhaps ten tables. Two British soldiers, who were the only customers, looked up as we entered, and then turned back to their beer. Two rather young bulbous Jewish women, perhaps twenty-five years old, appeared, and, hesitating a moment to recognize that we were Americans, rushed forth with profuse greetings, cooings and leering, and proceeded to talk to us into our chairs as we quizzically raised an eyebrow at each other.

Swetland in a jaunty manner grinned, and said, "Well, fellas, I think I'll run along now."

Jerry grabbed him before he could take a step.

"Look," he said, "You don't have to drink, but in numbers there's strength," Then looking at the smiling, greasy face of the girl; who was practically nose to nose with him, he added, "I think."

There was Palestinian beer and brandy and gin, none of which sounded appetizing, but since we were seated and guarded, we ordered anyway. One of the girls turned on a music box somewhere and then sauntered up, rubbing her hands, and asked if we didn't want to dance. I felt rather lame, and smiled my apology. From the noises the other three made, I thought they'd broken their legs on the spot. It didn't take long to finish the drinks and bow ourselves out.

Down on King's Way, we found a much nicer looking place called the Vienna Café. There was a good orchestra music coming from upstairs, so we went, and took one of the few vacant tables. The floorshow was on, and seemed to be made up of Greeks, who put on a pretty fair performance. When it was over, the music played for dancing. The couples were mostly English officers and local civilian men and women. One of the dancers from the floorshow was a pretty blond girl with whom I was able to get a dance. As was the style, she danced practically a full arm's length away, but nonetheless she seemed to enjoy the dance as much as I did, and I was able to chisel her followers out of two or three more. To be able to dance with someone so enjoyable amid the scent of feminine perfume was a real thrill. I decided that her dancing should be Americanized a little, so I pulled her closer and managed to cut the space between us down to six or eight inches. That was fairly easily done, so later I tried again. Success! She looked up graciously as she closed the gap between us, and just as I was beginning to glow with the success of my operations, she gave me a sharp gasp and jumped back with a quick look of surprise. I didn't understand and was about to ask what the trouble was when the music ended, and she excused herself abruptly. I was indignant at her ill manners and thought about giving chase and telling her what I thought, but I calmed down and decided to let it pass.

As I turned to my table, I felt what the trouble had been. Beneath my shirt was my concealed stiletto whose handle had prodded her. I wonder if she ever raised enough nerve to dance with another American.

Across the small bay to the north form Haifa and about two miles south on the black top road from our camp, was the ancient city of Acre that is mentioned in the Bible. Here the Turks withstood the siege of Napoleon in 1799 and the siege of the Crusaders in 1191. About a mile northeast of the walls is a man-made hill from which Napoleon conducted his campaign against the town. Its water supply comes from the range of mountains twenty miles to the north, the border between Palestine and Syria. The water is brought all the way by an aqueduct that now stands on twenty-foot pillars and now goes just below the ground as it levels the hills and valleys in its path. The lines of the aqueduct are softened by growths of grass and vines, except where new stones have been added to replace fallen ones. The duct is open on top most of the way, and only in occasional places has it any leaks. These tend to cement themselves closed as the water evaporates and leaves its deposit of calcium salts. Outside the northern wall of the town is a newer portion of Acre, where the Mayor lives, and this was declared out-of-bounds to troops after some Australians, on a tear one evening, broke into the Mayor's harem and tried to order beer. The details of the escapade were not known. We learned to love the Australians for the hell they raised.

The city is walled only on the north and east because it is even better protected on the south and west by the sea breaking ceaselessly over flat reefs. The walls are in two parts with a dry moat between. On the corner of the higher inner walls is a prison that is still being used. Along the low sea wall are several of the old, short, bulgy cannons that were used for defense.

The 6,000 inhabitants of Acre live in a maze of attached buildings that look like one construction in a state of agonized contortion. In and under that structure of plaster and wood and stone with its off-level angles, are dirty, dank, smelly, little cobblestone paths shared by animals and people alike. On the walls that line the passageways are narrow balconies, and sometimes enclosed, connecting halls arch overhead. According to the law of the Turks, a man who owned on both sides of the street could connect his property as long a he left room for the passage of a camel with a full load of straw. In a small opening of the buildings that served partially as the towns market, fishermen repaired their nets and boats, and there stood the town's small white-domed mosque. It was the only clean looking structure in town. In the fashion of the East, the wall that extended partway around the mosque had broken pieces of glass bottles imbedded in cement on top to turn away would-be intruders..

I'm not a religious man in the sense of having deep faith in the Bible verbatim. There are many things that I honestly don't know. I see conclusive proof neither for nor against God's projecting Himself into earthly affairs. And yet, in spite of my lack of confirmed opinion and knowledge, the historic sights of Jerusalem proved profoundly awesome. More so, perhaps for me, than for someone who had better knowledge of exactly what to expect in the Holy City, because that trip cemented in place the odd bits of information which were a religious muddle in my mind.

Jerusalem is both old and new; a page of brittle yellow paper, and a white glazed sheet of colorful advertisement. On the north, east, and west of the old city is the modern Jerusalem, place of world politics, big modern stone buildings, electricity, and automobiles. And in one corner is the old walled city that has been demolished and rebuilt, re-conquered and re-freed. It is the capitol of a country and the birthplace of Christ. There have been so many battles among Christians that Moslems now hold the most ancient site and the old sacrificial rock of Israel, as well as the keys to the Church of The Holy Sepulcher, which is the center of Greek, Armenian, and Catholic worship. But the endless turmoil and destruction in Jerusalem has clouded with dust and uncertainty the landmarks of Christ's time mentioned in the Bible. Now; after the soldiers of the Jews, Babylonians, Macedonians, Greeks, Romans, Turks, English, and French, Americans visit the Holy City.

The four of us had obtained a four-day pass together. The taxi ride from Haifa was a distance of about seventy-five miles and cost each of us 700 mils, or about $11. We checked into the modern Eden Hotel at tea time and amused the waiters by ordering three sets of cakes with one tray of tea -- we had had no lunch.

After tea, we planned to walk the streets and get acquainted with the town. For some reason, the sidewalks were so crowded that people spilled over into the streets, and everywhere we went, the only word we could understand was "Americans". The American uniform was strange in this inland city.

It was beginning to grow dark, when an Arab dressed in European trousers and vest and a tarboosh, accosted us. Ordinarily we would walk past such a person, but his line sounded a little different. He wanted to be our guide to the city. Tomorrow he would meet us anywhere anytime.

"Good guide. Not cost much."

We were shaking our heads and turning away, when he remembered there was a special service about to take place in the Church of the Holy Sepulcher. We thought about that for a minute, held a consultation, and decided that in spite of the way our feet felt, we shouldn't risk missing something special, and so we followed the Arab.

I don't really know what I expected to find, and the trip to our destination maintained my suspense. Our guide moved rapidly, glancing back frequently to see if we were following. The four of us, strung out about seventy-five feet apart ducked in and around the crowd popping up on tiptoes at intervals to spot the head of the man proceeding. The street went downhill, and where it turned, we went straight ahead through what I would have believed was a hole between buildings had not the guide pointed up and said, "This Jaffa Gate of Old Wall."

The news was flung over successive shoulders as we sped on through the posts that were built to restrict all passers but men and animals. The street became narrow and the footing on the worn decline of bricks more difficult. On the left an opening appeared filled with beams that formed a support for an old brick wall that showed signs of being decrepit. We descended a series of low steps, passed between the beams and entered the Church of The Holy Sepulchre. The nave had a worn stone floor and was barren except for a small ornamented building in the center, we sped past to the raised deep chancel at the end of the room. Here, too, the floor was of worn stone. The room was dim except for the light from several banks of candles on an altar we were approaching. A long file of monks, clad in black robes took their places before the altar. They chanted in a low tone and turned to watch us. Our guide took us practically into their midst and began to explain what the meaning of the ceremony was. I felt embarrassed that he talked as the ceremony proceeded, but it seemed to bother no one but us Americans. There were a few other visitors in the shadows, but they seemed to be carrying on their own worship silently. As they finished they glanced up to examine us and stayed to watch the monks as we were doing.

The only furniture in the entire room belonged to the altar. On the platform was a simple, but massive wooden table about six feet long. On the table were two tapestries of rich design, but their color was lost in the dim light of a seven-place candelabrum of beautifully ornate gold and colored glass. In the recess behind the altar were the most beautiful works of art that I have ever seen. On either side are two full-length gold icons of the Virgin Mary. The gleaming gold of Her flowing robe reaches from Her throat to the ground. Her hands and face are beautifully tinted plaster, and the features are graciously lifelike. A tall sparkling tiara reaches almost to Her shoulders. In the center and a trifle more recessed than the first icons is a tender, stately painting of Christ, lavishly treated with gold and soft colors.

The worship service, which we discovered took place every evening, ended shortly, and we returned to our hotel without engaging the guide for tomorrow.

Early the next morning we came again to this church with a guide obtained through the hotel. At first I was confused by the beauty and religious history of this place, and the apparent indifference on the part of those whose life was devoted to worship there.

Mr. Howdy, our short, affable Greek guide, was very thorough and honest in his work. He was a spry little man who, from the coming grayness of his hair and bushy mustache and the soft lines in his face, I judged to be in his fifties. With business-like precision, we started our tour where we had started it the night before -- at the churches, but this time the explanation was much more interesting. Never did Mr. Howdy say that such and such an event had taken place on a certain spot when "it is believed that it happened here" was more honest. While the Protestants believe Calvary is outside Jerusalem to the north, the Catholics, Greeks, and Armenians insist it stands adjacent to the Sepulcher.

Standing before the altar of the Church of the Holy Sepulchre, Mr. Howdy told us that the gold icons had been a gift of the Russian church, and he retold the centuries of struggle that had taken place over rights of worship at this spot where the Cross had stood. For years the different sects could reach no amicable agreement as to who should keep the keys to the church, and when one sect locked the building, another would come in through a window and hold a secret service. Officials of Jerusalem finally turned the keys over to the Moslems, and they still hold them. Queen Helena of

Byzantine, as is true of many historic places in Jerusalem, rebuilt this church.

On a table near one of the gold icons of the Virgin, She is represented again in life-size bust with a sword piecing her heart. The features are beautiful and soft and sorrowful. In the glass case, which contains it, lie treasures of every variety from people in all walks of life. There are precious stones, rings, pendants, brooches, pins, watched, medals, necklaces -- anything of value that someone has felt moved to give. At times the gifts must be taken to a safe to make room for others.

Like most Protestants, I came to this place intending to hold aloof, if not to scoff, but the meaning that this spot holds for people the world over began to take hold of me. The grasp was faltering at first. Mr. Howdy pointed to the stone floor at the foot of the altar. If you lift that stone and put your hand down in there, you can feel the center of one of three squares cuts in the rock. It is the one that held the cross. I felt strangely moved, but I could not force myself to feel that cut in the rock, whether spurious or not. I wanted to touch this history, but it seemed sacrilegious to do so. Here could be material proof and I was afraid to show that I needed it. I held back, and Mr. Howdy turned away from the altar to the Church of the Holy Sepulchre. His action was not quite like turning away from a puppy that you are powerless to save from starving, but the way his eyes lingered as his face turned away, came back to me later, when he expressed his opinion of this tourist with a courteous remark. In the days of life-exhausting pilgrimages, the visitors to the Holy City were disappointed that there was so little of material evidence to repay them for their journey, so the monks created signs to satisfy them. After centuries of confusion, it is now difficult to discern the real from the false.

On land belonging to the sect of monks known as the White Fathers, there was an excavation prior to building their new church. Below five layers of civilization they had found the pool of Bethesda, where Christ is believed to have preformed his first miracles. Only a small part of the pool was uncovered, but for me the pool was not the startling thing. Visible to my eye as it never had been in a textbook, were five separate layers of humanity totaling fifty feet in depth. They represented 2,000 years. Why had rubble filled in the pool of Bethesda so that a succeeding generation built its home ten feet above? Hat it been done by the fury of war or the fury of nature? Whatever the answer, it had apparently occurred five times, and on the present day layer, an Arab woman was engaged in hanging out her washing.

In the old temple area of the Israelites, there stood a sacrificial stone, and the temple surrounding it is said to have been the place from which Jesus drove the moneychangers. Although the Bible indicates that Abraham took Isaac away from town to offer him to God, people say the sacrificial stone is the site of that offering. In the place of the Jewish temple stands the grandiose Temple of Omar -- beautiful outside, but a "killing" goes on inside. Following, a trifle more bluntly than in the Christian churches, the plan of progression nearer to the Divine for a fee, the priests of the Mosque will allow you to descend into the pit which contains the rock from which Mohammed is said to have ascended to Heaven.

Some of the Orthodox Jews believe that this large temple area in which the Mosque of Omar stands, once contained the Holy of Holies of the Jewish Temple, but since the exact spot is not known, they dare not venture inside for fear of treading on it. Consequently the religious place of the Jews is the great stone Wailing Wall just outside the area. Here the Chosen People wail from their Hebrew wailing books, not for themselves but for the lost power and glory of the Hebrew race. Small oil lamps are lighted in the crevices of the wall for friends who could not make the pilgrimage, and the sound which comes from this length of street is modulated but discordant chant of many devout people. Only occasionally do the wails grow emotional and tremulous.

Adjacent to the Garden of Gethsemane, which is within sight of Jerusalem at the foot of the Mount of Olives, stands a beautiful new church of All Nations. Its roof is divided into approximately twelve domes, the funds for which were contributed by Catholic organizations in different countries. One of the monks was from Kansas, and it was like old home week for him just to see an American. He escorted us around the church and showed us several arches and sections of floor that had been part of the early Crusader Church there. Outside was a lovely garden of flowers with paths among young olive trees. The only tree that remained from the Garden of Gethsemane was a bent and limbless trunk.

All through our trip, Paul and Ed showed the same discomfiture that I felt in the presence of religious ceremony, while Jerry being Catholic, was at ease. He placed lighted candles on the altars and crossed himself with the same easy sweeping motion the monks used. The other three of us felt that we were outsiders.

From the church of All Nations, we took a car over a mountain road toward the Dead Sea. At every strategic point along the road were tank traps built of cement cones. They were usually placed where a bridge could be blown out, and their presence made it impossible for a tank to go around. At the north end of the Dead Sea are large open areas where the seawater is dried so that its salts can be collected. The estimated wealth of the dissolved salts in the Dead Sea runs into millions of dollars. The dimensions of the sea are forty-seven by ten miles

We had brought our bathing suits for the express purpose of dunking in the famously buoyant water, and dunk we did. It was necessary to keep our heads out of the water, however, and even where my neck was slightly irritated from shaving the water stung severely. But the buoyancy was amazing. It was like sitting in quicksilver. Not far from us a man was actually lying high enough in the water that he had an umbrella propped up against one shoulder and was reading a book. When we came out, our skins were greasy to the touch.

The rivers, which contribute to the Dead Sea, wash through deep gorges to join the Jordan River before depositing their salts in this basin 1300 feet below sea level. The salt content of the water is 12% by weight.

From the Dead Sea we drove north to Jericho, from which there was no impression to be derived except amazement that it was this barren piece of land which the Jews wanted for farming. In time I had become more familiar with the Jewish side of the Palestine problem than with the Arab's. Although the Arabs owned and operated large fruit and truck farms, these were on good land with relatively simple irrigation problems. It became difficult for Jews to obtain good coastal land so they went to work on some of the rocky and arid portions. This area near Jericho and the Jordan rivers was about a million acres of alkaline desert. The Arab who owns it intended no use for the land, but steadfastly refused to sell it to a group of young Jews who had a plan to make it arable.

In the afternoon, we went back over the mountain road and traveled fifteen miles south of Jerusalem to Bethlehem. Everywhere rosaries and mother-of-pearl crosses were offered for sale. All items had "Bethlehem" stamped on them, and this reminded me of the time I had bought a tiny pair of beaded Indian moccasins in Wisconsin with "Green Bay, Wis." stamped on them.

The dilapidated brick building enclosing the Manger had been used as a stable between the last Crusades and a later time when a French King journeyed there. He was angered by the use the building was put to and had the entrance made so small that only humans could enter by bowing their heads.

The manger and the Grotto of The Nativity is as bright a spot in the colorless Church of the Nativity as The Star must have been on the night of Christ's birth. Rich trappings, polished marble, and beautifully ornate lamps surround the area.

It was in the Church of The Nativity that Mr. Howdy told me of seeing a group of Italian war prisoners being taken through the church. When the group started to leave, one of the men dropped behind. Mr. Howdy watched him gouge a bit of plaster from the wall and then rejoin his fellows.

"That bit of plaster," he said, "will mean more to that boy years from now than most tourists ever felt when visiting The Holy Land."

I remembered the look Mr. Howdy had given me that morning in the Church of The Hold Sepulcher, and I knew one of the tourists he referred to.

One of the last spots we visited that day was the rich and lovely Roman Catholic Church stands over the First Station of The Cross where Christ was turned over to the mob. It was an awesome feeling to be standing on those same cobblestones, though they were scoured now as they had never been in His day. Against one wall stands a wooden cross on which the sisters inscribed the names of anyone who wants to leave something of himself at that place. Knowing that it would mean a great deal to a close friend of mine at home, I had her name and her daughter's inscribed on the cross.

On the opposite wall a piece of cloth is framed. Barely discernable on the cloth are the lines of a face more gracious and beautiful and all knowing than human features can be. The sisters say that the cloth was used to cover Christ's face when He was taken from The Cross. The cloth, with no markings on it, had been kept through the centuries until someone conceived the idea of looking at it with x-ray. It was then that the lines were seen and made permanent.

I did not know whether to accept this story as fact or fiction. There are other stories of similar nature to be heard in Jerusalem.

The longer we stayed in Palestine, the longer we felt the historic pressure of the past ages that was a part of the people and their habits and their cities and countryside. The very land shows its age. There are no jagged mountains. The soft stone has al been worn down by the passage of human feet, the torrents of seasonal rain, and the grinding of wind-driven sand. The earth is so rocky that I could present only discouragement to most American farmers; and the soil has given until it will barely support the most hardy of growing things without fertilization. The earth of the hills is, for a great part washed down into the lowest valleys. Low, bald, worn hills are a common sight, and over this little desolate country the Jews and Arabs continue to fight even during the wartime. They will doubtless fight more fiercely when the war is over and money begins to grow scarce again. It is true that the Jews have made good farm and fruit lands out of much of the area where the Arabs, too, were irrigating and tilling successfully, but the Jews have also attacked the hopeless-looking rocky areas and the desert sections to make food grow.

If the Jews had the country to do with as they pleased, I have little doubt that they could make a prosperous and fruitful land of it, but the Arabs cannot be removed from their rightful home. There are many wealthy and progressive Arabs who also want to make a fine country out of Palestine, but they must drag with them a larger population of uneducated, underfed, and uninterested fellows.

In seeing the filth and prevalent disease of this region, it occurred to me that these people are being retarded in their rightful progress, because the strength of their bodies and minds must combat disease. The flies swarm over everything -- over food and latrines and animals and people. You brush them off, and they are right back about their business before the motion is even completed. The flies, in their aggressiveness, actually try to pry themselves into your mouth unless you constantly brush them away. When a wanderer lies asleep on the streets of a city, he wraps himself closely to his dirty cloth to keep out those insects, and the little children run about with open sores on their faces and bodies covered by unmolested flies.

In many ways Palestine is a modern country. Its industries and managers have come from Europe, but its workmen have come from the open country. They have not lived together in large numbers until working in the cities compensated for the crowding. We Westerners have had to learn sanitation and establish laws for working in large groups as we built larger industries and moved together in greater numbers. In Palestine, we have brought our oil refining and have built up the furniture and silk and spices trade for our own benefit. But we have done little to help the people in their problems of living together, for live together they must to produce what we want. It takes money for compulsory education and for good wholesale sanitation, but we don't want to spend it, because such expenditures are not worthwhile to us? Partly that may be true, because with education the prices of labor would rise, but also the expenditures would have to be made now while the results would not show for several generations. It would be hard to show in black and white what the return on such an investment would be. Monetary return is still the scale by which we measure progress. People have not yet come to weigh progress by the long run while they must still live their lives by the short run. And so men will lie on the streets of Haifa and pull their dirty cloths around them to keep off swarms of disease-laden flies, and the Arabs will hold arid land that the Jews would cultivate.

A good portion of the Palestine troubles exists because two peoples were promised a land by someone who did not own it. But England is showing signs of fighting off the clutches of her historic past wherein a little island ruled with trade and force a great many lands on the face of the earth. Some of the policies may have smelled of old musty pigeon holes in an antique desk, but perhaps the rebuilding of post-war Britain will include new desks and fresh pigeon holes, for her people are truly fine -- and I trust they are able to solve the problems of America as glibly as we settle theirs.

One day at noon Ed had a sly smile on his face.

"How would you like a trip to India?" he asked

When Ed smiled with a touch of a leer at the corner of his mouth where he tried to hold back full grin, he meant what he said.

"Heck yes," I answered. "When do we go?"

"I don't know exactly. Three crews will go out of our whole group to form a new outfit in India. The Major said we had first choice. They'll decide who goes tomorrow, and we should leave pretty soon."

It was so easy that Gimble was positive we were being shanghaied out. He felt sure the Major held some of his earlier action against him -- stealing his girl and showing disrespect to his commanding officer. But we weren't being shanghaied -- we volunteered, and because of Ed's position in the squadron he had the first choice after two others turned down the offer.

Two of the crews selected were at St. Jean, and we were all given a four-day leave together. I had known the other officers by sight, but this was the first time we were thrown together. Sometimes you pick up friends one at a time as events of successive days draw you together and cement your relationship with mutual interests and appreciations. But the eight of us became friends quickly on the unsettled soil of a common but unknown future.

The pilot of the other crews, Henry Root, was little -- a mischievous, black-haired boy, whose ear-to-ear grin was a personality all its own. It frolicked for its own amusement. It looked at someone and won a friend, or atrophied into a small-pursed line of painful solemnity, if there was an overseeing frown to hold the tight little line in place. Henry and his co-pilot, Ted Williams, looked like a bulldog pup and a palm tree. Ted was tall, slender, and graceful. His arms were so long that he frequently frightened himself upon waking to find an arm reaching over his left shoulder and a hand dangling over his face. When he gained nerve enough to grab the foreign hand with his left one, he found it was his own right hand and arm, which had wound behind his head while he slept. Ted's long, lined face looked like an impossible drawing board for the full friendly smile that frequently re-lined it. Their bombardier was Henry's size, but more wiry. He was sagacious, quiet Mike Ryan. Montez, the navigator, was the young counterpart of Cesar Romero, the movie star -- black and curly hair, long thin mustache, and Latin features.

We were allowed an Army reconnaissance car for our leave. Gimble couldn't be found when it was time to go on our sightseeing trip, so the other seven of us put on clean khaki and "pinks", and with Henry Root herding our car with its wobbly front end toward the Syrian border, we started our last view of the Near East.

After twenty miles, the blacktop curved out to the Mediterranean and climbed to the cut end of the low mountain barrier that separates Syria from Palestine. Here sits the "Duane", or French customs. Between it and the sea runs the single track of the railroad. We passed the civil inspector, flashed our passes at the British Military Police, and sped on into Grande Leban—the Lebanon State of Syria. We passed orange and banana-farms, closeted in high stonewalls, and off to the left, apparently sitting out on the waters of the sea was the low, battered town of Tyre. No longer is there Phoenician wealth of "Babylon and Tyre." Farther on, above Sidon (now called Saida), were a few demolished buildings and shell craters where the French had held up the British at a bridge when Syria was taken in 1940.

At a road junction just outside Beyruit, I recalled something that made me chuckle. On an earlier trip to Beyruit, I had come to this place to hitchhike back to Palestine, but I was not sure which road I should travel. Squatting by the side of the road was an old Arab, simply watching the world go by. I knew that asking directions in English would be of no use, but I thought by mentioning Haifa and pointing down both roads he would correct me.

I pointed, saying, "Which way is Haifa?"

The old man suddenly came alive and jumped to his feet. His face was wreathed in smiles and throwing his arms joyfully in the air as though greeting a long-lost brother, said in perfect English, "You speak American!"

It seemed strange to hear "you speak American!" instead of "You speak English!" He said he had run a tailor shop in New York. Business grew bad, so he came home. For the last ten years he had been damning himself for his foolishness, because now he had no money to go back.

On the former trip here, I had arrived late at night, and the hotels seemed to be closed up. In the center of town I found a place to sleep on the roof of a Presbyterian hostel for soldiers. I wakened with the first lifting of night. A soft ringing of bells seemed to come vibrantly from all directions. At first I thought it was my ears ringing. Then came the droning recital of nasal sounds as a nearby Muezzin summoned the faithful to prayer. I felt a warm glow of satisfaction inside my body. It was like a little boy waking to find himself a character in the Arabian Nights. I was not a little disappointed when I found that the skyline of Beyruit was built of square corners, not of domes and minarets.

This afternoon, we checked in at the Regent Hotel, and Ed and I went to the home of the Rubinskys for dinner. They were a family of white Russians with whom my sister and her husband had lived several years before when they taught at the American University of Beyruit. It was to see these people that I had hitchhiked to Beyruit earlier. Dr. Rubinsky is a tall, partially bald teacher of physics. He is friendly and quiet and sincere. His English has a Russian vibrancy to it, but is fairly easy to understand. Dr. Rubinsky years ago, did some initial work on the bombsight that we have used in our low level bombers in this war. His wife, as did he, fairly bubbled with joy at seeing this brother of her loving friend, the American "Katia", as she called my sister Kate. Madame Rubinsky still looked distinguished in spite of worry and hard work. Frequently my remarks taxed her knowledge of English to the point where she would have to turn to her slim, lovely, 12 year old daughter, Tania, for an explanation, and it would come forth more beautifully than an American could make it. The two boys, Andre and Usha, seventeen and eighteen years, are honor students in physics and will go to an American school where they hope to be trained in aeronautical engineering. And grandmother Rubinsky was just as my sister had described her -- standing in the kitchen, muttering into a steaming pot of cabbage! Sometimes, when she would spout a Russian sentence at us, gracious, alert little Tanyia would turn to her pleasantly with a Russian answer, and then return her attention to us.

Ed was as thoroughly impressed with this unassuming, noble family as I was. They were people living on a small income, devoted to the faithful pursuit of knowledge, and enjoying together their search.

The following day the morning paper announced that General Montgomery had broken the German line at El Alamein. The British Intelligence had told us Rommel had sixteen days of gas, then eight, then four. After that, there had been ten days of silence, and now the break had come.

After breakfast, which included chewing a small cup of Turkish coffee, Ed, Swetland, and I roamed the streets of Beyruit, looking at Brocade, knives, and leather articles. In the afternoon, all of us were invited to the Rubinsky's for tea, and an elaborate one it was. They advised us what to see during the rest of our trip.

Following their suggestions, we drove over the coastal mountains, next day, and had lunch at Ryak in the interior valley. Ryak had been an important French airfield, but it had been partially sabotaged when the British were about to capture it. Now it was an American base that served as a repair depot for our planes in Palestine. We found many old friends there whom we hadn't seen since leaving the States.

From Ryak we drove twelve miles north to Baalbek, the ruins of three Roman temples to Jupiter, Venus, and Bacchus. The area is strewn with gigantic tumbled rocks, and in several places beautifully carved columns of stone rise approximately 125 feet. The cornices and rock segments that make up the columns are gigantic, and yet they are carved so well that it is not easy too find where the rocks join each other. There is a great subterranean passage beneath the whole area, and in one room is a plaster model of the temples as they were believed to have been.

Late in the afternoon, we went back down to the valley to take the road over barren hills to Damascus. The hills rose little more than 2000 feet. As we ascended the western slope, I looked at the dry and shrub-less surroundings and wondered what there was in this region that had maintained Damascus as the oldest and most important commercial city in this portion of the Near East.

Near the crest of the hills, I noticed a trickle of water beside the road. As we descended the far slope, the trickle grew larger, and small spots of green appeared. Then there were shrubs and trees, and the trickle was a river.

Entering Damascus was like leaving the tube of a funnel to enter the mouth. It was a large busy city with signs of age and youth in its buildings, transportation, and people.

We obtained rooms at the Oriental Palace Hotel, a spacious modern place where East met West in the music room which was ante-place to the dining hall. Music played and prosperous-looking Arabs and Europeans talked over their tea.

There is little which cannot be purchased in the Damascus bazaars. There are smells of spice, rope, leather, sweets, and many more than a westerner can recognize at first meeting. We bought brocades, knives, inlaid boxes, and other trinkets. In the silver market anything you desire of precious metal will be made before your eyes. This market is housed in a sprawling building of aged brick with a tin roof. The interior is broken up into small booths by rickety fencing that leaves a few narrow aisles. The booths are never locked, and yet from a drawer in one of them the proprietor pulled out and handed me a small but heavy brick of solid yellow gold.

We visited the factory that made inlaid boxes, and saw furniture we could have bought for $40, which would have sold for $200 in America -- but we had no way to get it safely home. There were card tables and desks and bedroom and living room furniture, all inlaid.

That night we wandered around the streets waiting for a particular nightclub to open. In one little dive, there was a stage in the corner of the room, on which an Arab girl sang accompanied by a man at a piano. She had on a flimsy brassier, and veil-like skirt, and she swayed her hips gently as she sang her song. Then, as she broke into the chorus, her hips bounced the "bumps" in the increased tempo, and the innocent expression on her face changed to a lascivious leer. The Arab men howled their approval, but all we could enjoy was the catchy rhythm of the chorus and the girl. We would have given anything to know what the words were.

At the modernistic nightclub farther down the street, the main attraction was a colored couple from Harlem. They danced a wild apache dance that would be good anywhere that it could be passed by the censor. The girl was a cute little person, light in color. When the floorshow broke up and all the dancers (the rest were white) came back for their dressing rooms, it was the colored girl who was the belle of the ball as far as the French and English officers were concerned. They lined up for the opportunity to dance with her.

On the road from Damascus to Tiberous, at the head of the Sea of Galilee (now called Lake Tiberous), we saw a long train of 300 camels coming in from the desert. The great animals were heavily loaded, but the little donkeys seemed to be carrying almost as much. The camels were in strings of ten or fifteen, tied together by lead ropes. Usually but one weather-browned Arab walked with a group of camels. I wondered exactly what filled the bulging hemp bags, but there was little chance of discovery since they these camel trains never trade their merchandise until they reached their destination. Seeing this long procession of stupid-looking camels with the loose skin of their lips hanging away from their teeth, and the faithful little donkeys plodding unharnessed, heads down I was reminded of a remark I had heard before leaving the States. Someone said there could be nothing wrong with the America First Committee. "Just look at all the big names connected with it!" The man with him said, "Did you ever see a camel train in the desert? For mile after mile you see nothing but big camels. And then you come to the head of the train, and what's that leading the whole thing? A little jackass!"

By nightfall, we were back at our base, and in a few days we boarded a DC-3 for India.

Trying to think back to the time just before we left for India -- and including the time--we were flying over the desert and blowing sand and water that lay before Karachi -- I can find few concrete prospects that I anticipated having fulfilled by India. Perhaps one was that at some time I expected to see an exquisitely rich and ornate temple partially lost in a tangle of jungle growth. I also knew that the Japs help Burma and so it was there that we would bomb. The rumors about what our position would be brought visions of Ed as a squadron commander and me as an operations officer.

At the close of this four months in Africa, I had no thoughts about the time yet to be spent away from home. In a sense, I was fed up with war and travel, and yet new lands and scenes were always intriguing. Had I known that four months would stretch to fourteen, and that two-thirds of the crews on that transport would never go home, I should have felt hopeless to the point of being physically sick. There were many times when the part we played in the whole drifted beyond my grasp, and I felt like just another coffee bean being ground to order.

9th Squadron

W. M. GILBERT, (F), A De-
Pauw man from Evanston, Illinois. Worked for Oscar–Mayer
Meat Packing Industry following a noteworthy degree in
Chemistry. A fellow who sees
things through to the end.

Air Corps Book

The Chicago Daily News – Oct 1942

How Yanks Bombed Axis In Greek Raid

With the U.S. Army Air Forces in the Middle East, Oct 8,1942 – On Saturday afternoon the thundering herd of American "Pink Elephants" appeared over Axis - occupied Greece, bombed shipping in Navarino Bay and shot down two Axis pursuit ships.

Not only that, but they threw the German Luftwaffe officer into a stuttering rage because the American boys wouldn't stop talking on the wave length the German was using to clear his fighters off the field.

Not only that, but thanks to courtesies extended to the press by everybody, from Gen Lewis H. Brereton on down, this correspondent was able to go along on the mission and for the first time in six years, to be on the dispatching end of the bombing instead of the reviewing end.

The "Pink Elephants" that struck the enemy in Europe in broad daylight and unescorted were big four engined B-24's of the heavy bomber group. Since their arrival out there the B-24'w have taken on a salmon complexion for camouflage purposes and they are sometimes collectively referred to as "Pink Elephants," but they retain the individual names they had before they left home.

First to Take Off

Leading us was Maj. John R. "Killer" Kane's "Hail Columbia" and his right wing "Eager Beavers," with an Evanston boy, William Gilbert as co-pilot. Following were other names that were to assert themselves over enemy territory later: "Snow White," "The Witch," "Jersey Jackals," "Alice the Goon," "Number Nine" and "Natchez to Memphis."

Illinois was represented in "Number Nine" by J.W. Wallace of Moline, Ill, and Chicago by Lt. B. N. Tully in "Snow White."

Looking over the shoulders of the pilot and co pilot sitting side by side, we got a clear view of the runway slipping fast beneath the plane, then dropping away as we rose and turned to join the formation with other bombers.

Behind us other elements were taking off and we circled the airdrome until they were well off the ground. The formation took shape, then went out to sea flying low over the blue water.

It was a long way to go, Navarino Bay on the Southwest coast of Peloponnesus and past Crete. Before the take off the crews had crowded into the briefing room for their instructions: Target, bombing altitude, route and return route. Our target we were told, were two ships in the Navarino Bay. We were to be careful not to confuse the elongated island in the middle of the bay with a ship.

EVANSTON BOY, CHICAGO FLIER IN GREEK RAID

Two Army fliers of the Chicago area took part in a raid on Axis shipping in a Greek harbor, it was disclosed today in Richard Mowrer's dispatch that gave an eye-witness account of the raid as seen from one of the bombers. They are Lt. William Gilbert of Evanston and Lt. B. N. Tully, 7655 S. Aberdeen st.

Lt. Gilbert, co-pilot of the "Eager Beavers" bomber in the raid over Greece, is a member of an Evanston family. He is an athlete, a stalwart six-footer, former member of the DePauw University football team. He was graduated from the University at Greencastle, Ind., in 1940 and is 24 years old.

He is the son of the late William C. Gilbert, an attorney. His mother, Mrs. Esther M. Gilbert, has been a leader in the Evanston Woman's Club, but at present is making her home with her sister, Mrs. Lynn Wheeler, 512 Park av., River Forest. The family lived in Evanston for years at 2516 Park pl.

Young Gilbert has been in the Army only 14 months. He left a Florida training field three months ago for overseas service.

Lt. Tully, an officer of the "Snow White" bomber, is the son of Michael J. Tully, a Surface Lines motorman on the Halsted st. line, and Mrs. Hannah Tully. He was a medical student at Loyola University, in his third year, when he enlisted, and he received his wings last July at Miami.

He was married at Miami to a nurse, Isabelle Connatt, who is now believed to be an Army nurse in Alaska.

WEATHER INDICATIONS
(United States Weather Bureau Forecast.)
Oct. 8, 1942.

Chicago and vicinity—Mild temperatures today. Slightly cooler tonight. Light winds becoming moderate to fresh this afternoon. Temperatures since 6 p. m. yesterday:

6 p.m.	73	7 a.m	53
8 p.m.	65	8 a.m	54
10 p.m.	58	9 a.m	55
12 midnight	55	10 a.m	66
2 a.m.	54	11 a.m	73
4 a.m.	54	12 noon	75
6 a.m.	52		

Sunrise, 6:57; sunset, 6:20; moon rises at 6:10 a. m. tomorrow.
(Additional weather data on page 32.)

How Yanks Bombed Axis In Greek Bay

BY RICHARD MOWRER.

SPECIAL CABLE
To The Chicago Daily News Foreign Service.
Copyright, 1942. The Chicago Daily News, Inc.

With the U.S. Army Air Forces in the Middle East, Oct. 8.—On Saturday afternoon a thundering herd of American "pink elephants" appeared over Axis-occupied Greece, bombed shipping in Navarino Bay and shot down two Axis pursuit ships.

Not only that, but they threw a German Luftwaffe officer into a stuttering rage because the American boys wouldn't stop talking on the wave length the German was using to clear his fighters off the field.

Not only that, but thanks to courtesies extended to the press by everybody, from Gen. Lewis H. Brereton on down, this correspondent was able to go along on the mission and, for the first time in six years, to be on the dispatching end of a bombing instead of the reviewing end.

The "pink elephants" that struck the enemy in Europe in broad daylight and unescorted were big four-engined B-24's of a heavy bomber group. Since their arrival out here the B-24's have taken on a salmon-pink complexion for camouflage purposes and they are sometimes collectively referred to as "pink elephants," but they retain the individual names they had before they left home.

First to Take Off.

This correspondent was assigned to the "Raunchy." With Maj. John R. "Killer" Kane's "Hail Columbia" and his right wing "Eager Beavers," we were the first element to take off. Looking over the shoulders of the pilot and co-pilot sitting side by side, we got a clear view of the runway slipping fast beneath the plane, then dropping away as we rose and turned to join the formation with other bombers.

Behind us other elements were taking off and we circled the airdrome until they were well off the ground. The formation took shape, then went out to sea, flying low over the blue water.

It was a long way to go, Navarino Bay on the southwest coast of Peleponnesus and past Crete. Before the takeoff the crews had crowded into the briefing room for their instructions: Target, bombing altitude, route and return route.

Our target, we were told, was two ships in Navarino Bay. We were to be careful not to confuse the small elongated island in the

Set Their Watches.

The men had set their watches and asked one or two more questions. Then the briefing was over and we had piled into trucks to be taken to our respective bombers. Ground crews standing around and ready, had reported on the condition of their planes. Engines had been warmed up. There was no delay and the takeoffs had been on schedule. The formation was complete as it flew low over the sea.

Leading us was Maj. Kane's "Hail Columbia" and on our right were the "Eager Beavers" with an Evanston boy, William Gilbert as co-pilot. Following were other names that were to assert themselves over enemy territory later: "Snow White," "The Witch," "Jersey Jackals," "Alice the Goon," "Number Nine" and "Natchez to Memphis."

Illinois was represented in "Number Nine" by J. W. Wallace of Moline, Ill., and Chicago by Lt. B. N. Tully in "Snow White."

It's Hot in Plane.

The sun pouring in through the glass roof of the cockpit was hot and perspiration trickled down the faces of both pilots as they watched the leading plane and checked the instrument panel. Pilot Lt. Leroy Williams Jr. of Jackson, Miss., took off his shirt, and pretty soon his co-pilot, Lt. Thomas S. Behr of Houston, Tex., followed suit.

Several hours later the free air temperature would be below freezing when we got to our bombing altitude, but right now it was hot. In the nose of the bomber, the navigator tested the forward guns. He was Lt. Joseph T. Houston of Floresville, Tex., the man who, on the recent high-altitude raid over Tobruk, had breathed oxygen and life back into the lungs of the subconscious Waist Gunner Holt whose oxygen mask had frozen.

The bombardier, also in the nose, checked the bombsight. Behind the pilots' seats sat the radio operator. Above was the power-driven top turret and all we could see of its occupant was a pair of shoes, garterless socks, white skin and the lower pants legs of blue coveralls turned up at the cuffs.

The power-driven turret purred as the top gunner tested it. The

(Continued on page 10, column 1.)

Greek Raid, Chicago Daily News, Oct 8, 1942

Gilbert Christmas 1960: Bill, Jeanette, Diana, Glenn, Kate, and Meryl

Cadet Gilbert during flight training in Tampa FL 1942

The Chicago Daily News – Nov. 1942

Rickenbacker Presents D.F.C. to
Lt. William Gilbert at India Base

Presentation of the Distinguished Flying Cross was made to Lieut. William M. Gilbert and nine other men by Eddie Rickenbacker recently in India, according to a letter received this week by aunt and uncle Mr. and Mrs. Barry Gilbert, 2653 Orrington Avenue. He is the son of Mrs. Esther M. Gilbert, formerly of 2516 Park Place, now visiting in Santa Rosa, CA.

"Quite a thrill and honor came to us," Lieut. Gilbert wrote, "when Eddie Rickenbacker stopped in at our field, still wobbly to pin the D.F.C. on 10 of us. He's a real man, with more vitality than three men, and although his hands shook when he pinned on the medal, when he grabbed me by the hand and looked squarely into my eyes and said, "I'm glad to know you," it was a real thrill.

"It was blazing hot, and all of us including Rickenbacker, were drenched with perspiration. Yet he insisted upon talking to us and telling us about his "21 days" and about conditions in other was theatres.

Award of the Distinguished Flying Cross was the second honor to come to Lieut. Gilbert in several months. Late in March or early in April he received the Air Medal from the hand of Gen. Hap Arnold, Chief of the Army Air Forces, having completed more than 100 hours of combat duty as a bomber pilot and co pilot. He has since been relieved of combat duty to avoid excessive strain and has been squadron communications officer.

A graduate of Evanston High School and of De Pauw, Lieut. Gilbert entered the Air Forces in August 1941. He went overseas in August, 1942 and was stationed in Syria before going to India in December.

Rickenbacker Presents D.F.C. to Lt. William Gilbert at India Base

Presentation of the distinguished flying cross was made to Lieut. William C. Gilbert and nine other men by Eddie Rickenbacker recently in India, according to a letter received this week by his aunt and uncle, Mr. and Mrs. Barry Gilbert, 2653 Orrington avenue. He is the son of Mrs. Esther M. Gilbert, formerly of 2516 Park place, now visiting in Santa Rosa, Cal.

"Quite a thrill and honor came to us," Lieut. Gilbert wrote, "when Eddie Rickenbacker stopped in at our field, still burned and wobbly, to pin the D.F.C. on 10 of us. He's a real man, with more vitality than three men, and although his hands shook when he pinned on the medal, when he grabbed me by the hand and looked squarely into my eyes and said, 'I'm glad to know you,' it was a real thrill.

"It was blazing hot, and all of us, including Rickenbacker, were drenched with perspiration. Yet he insisted upon talking to us and telling us about his '21 days' and about conditions in other war theaters."

Award of the distinguished flying cross was the second honor to come to Lieut. Gilbert in several months. Late in March or early in April he received the air medal from the hand of Gen. "Hap" Arnold, chief of the army air forces, having completed more than 100 hours of combat duty as bomber pilot and co-pilot. He has since been relieved of combat duty to avoid excessive strain and has been made squadron communications officer.

A graduate of Evanston High school and of De Pauw, Lieut. Gilbert entered the air forces in August, 1941. He went overseas in August, 1942, and was stationed in Syria before going to India in December.

Rickenbacker presents D.F.C. to Lt. Willliam Gilbert

B.E. Smith, Jim Pederson, Dick Lowman, Fay Francis
Moran, Hank Gober, Bill Gilbert

BAIN PHOTO SERVICE
Oxnard, Calif.
Nov. 1, 1941

Oxnard Field Crew names

Oxnard Training

Gilbert family 1920: Kate, William C., William M., Esther and Esther's sister, bother-in-law and mother Miller: Mary Jane McKean Miller, descendant of Thomas McKean, signer of the Declaration of Independence. Mary McKean Miller's husband, Reverend Amos Miller, a Methodist minister, fought in the Civil War and was commissioned to write "The History of the Thirteenth Illinois Infantry, pub. 1892.

William Gilbert and Faith Philips, good friends, Plaza del Lago, Wilmette, IL

William Gilbert #33, tackle, for De Pauw University football team

GILBERT, WILLIAM McKEAN
Evanston, Illinois
Chemistry. BΘΠ;
Chemistry Club; "D"
Association; Football,
1, 2, 3, 4; Track, 1,
2, 3.

William Gilbert - plays tackle #33 for De Pauw Universtiy Football

William Gilbert and mother, Esther Gilbert at cabin on Torch Lake

William Gilbert at Mather Field March 1942

THE CHICAGO DAILY NEWS – JUNE 24, 1942

Chicago Bomber Crews Cited As Greatest Outfit in India

Eighteen men from the Chicago area are members of a heavy bomber group with the 10th Air Force command in India which has been singled out by Maj. Gen. Clayton L Bissell, 10th Air Force commander, as an exemplary fighting unit, it was revealed today in an Associated Press dispatch.

Cited by President

Only a few days ago the group also learned of another citation issued in the name of the President---"for outstanding performance of duty in action during the period Jan. 14, to March 1, 1942"

"Opposing the full force of the numerically superior Japanese with all available aircraft." The citation said, "the bombardment group participated daily in attacking the enemy wherever it found him during his prolonged drive through the Philippines and Netherlands Indies to Java."

Superior courage Praised

"Long-range bombing attacks were executed in the face of heavy anti-aircraft fire and large concentrations of enemy fighter airplanes over the target areas. Despite extremely adverse weather and dangerous field conditions, hampered by lack of adequate personnel to maintain aircraft in continuous combat condition, many successful missions were performed by crew fatigued from daily fights against the numerically dominant enemy. The superior courage and devotion to duty shown by this bombardment group will always be worthy of emulation."

So far this year the bombardment unit has been bettering its records month by month. During the first 22 days of May the group rained 700 tons of high explosives on more than 40 targets.

Men from Chicago Area

Men from the Chicago area in the group include:

Lt. William Gilbert, son of Mrs. Esther M. Gilbert 512 Park Ave, River Forest; Lt. John Sanderson, Evanston; Lt. Raymond Ziegmont Chicago; Lt. Robert Shimanek 248 Wolcott Av. Lt. Arthur Flesch, 1035 W. Lill Av.; Lt. Joseph Coambs, 914 Sherman Av. Evanston; Sgt. Alfonse Ceislak, Chicago; Tech. Sgt Royal Peterson, Chicago; Staff Sgt. Theodore Malacha, Downers Grove; Tech Sgt. Russell Sibulski, Berwyn; Tech Sgt. Norman Goldstein, whose wife Francis lives at 5943 S Cornell Av. Agt. John Calla, Chicago; Staff Agt. Frank Holstein, Wheaton; Staff Sgt. Edward Girman, Whiting; Staff Sgt. Charles Kiesel, Cicero; and Staff Sgt. Matthew Olk, Evanston.

Among other Illinois men who are members of the group is Lt. Leland Berlette of Normal.

The Chicago Daily News – June 24

THE CHICAGO DAILY NEWS

Chicago Bomber Crews Cited As Greatest Outfit in India

Eighteen men from the Chicago area are members of a heavy bomber group with the 10th Air Force Command in India which has been singled out by Maj.Gen. Clayton L. Bissell, 10th Air Force commander, as an exemplary fighting unit, it was revealed to-day in an Associated Press dispatch.

"You men of this heavy bomber group have made a glorious record during the months you have been fighting the Japs in Burma and Thailand," Gen. Bissell recently told members of the unit. "I'd stack your group against any heavy bomber group in the world any time—and be confident of the results."

Cited by President.

Only a few days ago the group also learned of another citation—issued in the name of the President—"for outstanding performance of duty in action during the period Jan. 14 to March 1, 1942."

"Opposing the full force of the numerically superior Japanese with all available aircraft," the citation said, "the bombardment group participated daily in attacking the enemy wherever it found him during his prolonged drive through the Philippines and Netherland Indies to Java.

Superior Courage Praised.

"Long-range bombing attacks were executed in the face of heavy anti-aircraft fire and large concentrations of enemy fighter airplanes over the target areas. Despite extremely adverse weather and dangerous field conditions, hampered by lack of adequate personnel to maintain aircraft in continuous combat condition, many successful missions were performed by crews fatigued from daily flights against the numerically dominant enemy. The superior courage and devotion to duty shown by this bombardment group will always be worthy of emulation."

So far this year the bombardment unit has been bettering its records month by month. During the first 22 days of May the group rained 700 tons of high explosives on more than 40 targets.

Men from Chicago Area.

Men from the Chicago area in the group include:

Lt. William Gilbert, son of Mrs. Esther M. Gilbert, 512 Park av., River Forest; Lt. John Sanderson,

WM. GILBERT. ART. FLESCH.

L. BERLETTE. JOS. COAMBS.

Flesch, 1035 W. Lill av.; Lt. Joseph Coambs, 914 Sherman av., Evanston; Sgt. Alfonse Ceislak, Chicago; Tech. Sgt. Royal Peterson, Chicago; Staff Sgt. John Jaeger, Chicago; Staff Sgt. Theodore Malacha, Downers Grove; Tech. Sgt. Russell Zeiss, Downers Grove; Staff Sgt. Russell Sibulski, Berwyn; Tech. Sgt. Norman Goldstein, whose wife, Frances, lives at 5943 S. Cornell av.; Sgt. John Calla, Chicago; Staff Sgt. Frank Holstein, Wheaton; Staff Sgt. Edward Girman, Whiting; Staff Sgt. Charles Kiesel, Cicero; and Staff Sgt. Matthew Olk, Evanston.

Among other Illinois men who are members of the group is Lt. Leland Berlette of Normal.

Missouri Floods Costly.

Jefferson City, Mo., June 24.—(P)—Floods and heavy rains have cost Missouri farmers $40,000,000 in lost crops this year, Agriculture Commissioner John W. Ellis estimated last night.

Lt. William Gilbert's unit receives Unit Citation

William M Gilbert, Tackle, #33 at DePauw University, JV football, 1938

GILBERT, WILLIAM McKEAN

Evanston, Illinois

Chemistry. BΘΠ;
Chemistry Club; "D"
Association; Football,
1, 2, 3, 4; Track, 1,
2, 3.

De Pauw Yearbook

Capt. William Gilbert in London flying for American Overseas Airlines, 1947.

Gilbert family at home 2516 Park Place, Evanston IL, 1936, Wm.
C. Gilbert, Esther, Wm. M Gilbert, and niece Jody Hanke

Chapter V

INDIA

In Karachi, India a young Colonel was reassembling men for his group of B-24's. With the start of the monsoon the previous June, his men had flown their B-17's to Africa, and now that the weather was again fit for flying, some of these men and some of us newer ones were coming back to fly in a longer range airplane.

We had very few duties the week or ten days we were at Karachi, so we spent most of the time seeing the town, the movies, going to dances at the English clubs and at the American Officers' club -- and becoming accustomed to the continual sight of half-starved beggars. We quickly found that if we gave a few annas to one, all the others would follow us, moaning, for blocks.

Gimble and Swetland were the first to discover, amid the heat and foreign atmosphere of this Eastern city, a busy little shop that called itself the Manhattan Ice Cream Parlor. The names of the dishes stumped us. There were such things as an Old Duchess sundae and a Dead Man freeze. Altogether there were fifty-one different combinations of ice cream, fruits, nuts, and syrups. This sudden exposure to ice cream went to our heads, and before we left Karachi, every one of them had been tried.

The shops held objects of metal, cotton, silk, ivory, and glass which we had seen nowhere else. We bought a great many fine gifts, but at nearly five times the usual price, because we were known to be Americans and could not bargain well.

Our mission in India was no more than a meager delaying action. The Japanese already had the Burma road, were chasing the Chinese back and forth across the Salween River northeast of Mandalay, and were providing pursuit attacks against our feeble air supply route over the Himalaya Mountains. If the transport pilots had clear weather, they could fly in the valleys and fly nearer the Japanese lines where the mountains were lower, but with bad weather, they had to fly above the highest altitudes of the terrain. The farther north they went to avoid the Japs, the higher they had to fly, and if the winds drifted them north of their course, or if their altimeters were not correct, they crashed into the mountains amid some of the most jagged terrain in the world. They were rarely heard of again. Even if a small plane sighted survivors near the wreckage, it was seldom that it could land to give assistance.

The most forward base that the Allies held was Chittagong, in Burma on the Bay of Bangal, about fifty miles north of the Jap-held city of Akyab. Burma was a gouging thumbs in the Allied eye, but it was not too solidly appended to other Japanese territory nearer their home bases. Almost all munitions, and possibly some food, had to come to Burma by boat from the direction of Singapore. The boats could unload at Moulmein and let their cargo proceed by rail for the remaining 200 miles to Pegu, north of Rangoon, but this was not the most efficient method. The ships could go directly to Rangoon where there were ample facilities for unloading and storage, or go up the Bassein River and be unloaded by smaller boats that could proceed to the rail terminal town of Bassein. The supplies could then go north by rail from Bassein to Myanaung on the Irriwassy, or north from Rangoon and Pegu through Mandalay to Mogaung. A parallel route to this one railroad was the river itself, on which were a great number of small boats propelled by both men and motors. Although they were only 200 miles apart, there was no supply connection between Bangkok in Thailand, and the Moulmein Railroad. The enemy did show signs of industry, however, east of Ye, below Moulmein, and we were sent to take strips photos of the area to see if a road of some sort was being put through. There were no signs of one at that time.

It was our job to bomb railroad bridges and marshalling yards, docks, warehouses, and the ships wherever they might be, in harbors or in their sea-lanes.

Our first base was at Gaya in central India, where the Buddha temple stands on the site of the spiritual awakening of Price Gautama. The field had been a small airways station and was converted to military use by the lengthening of the strips and the addition of native-built barracks. They were more comfortable quarters than we had expected. The buildings were in long strips of ten rooms, raised about a foot off the ground on a cement-covered base of rubble. The roof was of thick rice straw covered by thin, fragile tile made a few hundred feet away. The walls were of soft brick plastered over to give a stable appearance. This was misleading because they sometimes crumbled under the weight of small trees used as beams to hold the roof. In order that dust particles stirred up by the scurrying of rats and mice wouldn't drift down into the room, the ceilings were made flat with a sheet of gunny.

We found it interesting to watch the men squatting before their pottery wheels making our roof tile. One man worked the clay into the proper consistency, and then it was plopped in the center of the spinning wheel. The hands of the spinner squeezed the mound up into a cylinder. With the index and middle fingers pressing into the tip of the whirling cylinder, a thin wall of wet clay was formed against the thumb, which was held on the outside. When his whole hand was inside the cup formed, the man let a small piece of string wind itself around the column and cut off the proper length of tube. This was lifted off, lined with a stick on each side, and when dry from the sun, broken into two unbaked tile. All the halves were then arranged in a careful mound over a bed of coal, and the whole thing cemented over with clay. When the coal fire died out, the outside clay was broken off, and the red brittle tile was ready for the roof.

On our first mission, the Colonel took us to Mandalay to bomb the railway yards. The wild Chin Hills that form the barrier between India and Burma had a sudden appeal for all of us. The hills were about five thousands feet high and heavily wooded. There were streams visible in the valleys, and one great waterfall there was a fascinating sight as well as a landmark. It looked like a movie setting for one of Dorothy Lamour's bathing scenes. Sometimes, when we flew low over the hills on the way home, we could pick out a few bare spots that looked like parts of a trail, and occasionally there was thin blue smoke from a fire. I almost wished I could bail out over these hills sometime and spend the rest of the war finding my way home. Having since heard what it is like to be lost in the Chin Hills, I am very happy that my thoughts did not culminate in action.

Mandalay was in the second valley, and could be seen from a good distance away through the haze. We were at 16,000 feet and below at about 3000 feet was a broken cloud layer. As we neared the target, the suspense increased suddenly. We scanned the air above and below for enemy fighters. We were in three elements of three-ship Vs staggered down to the rear in "javelin" formation, as it was called. The formation tightened up, but not an enemy was in sight. We turned on the target for the bomb run-- it should be about a minute before the bombs fell. A minute passed. Three minutes passed, and Ed took his eyes off the PDI (Pilot's Direction Indicator) for brief instants to straighten up and peer earthward. His eyes peeking out over the oxygen mask glanced at me, at the formation ahead, at the PDI, at Mandalay below. Slowly the formation began to turn and circle the town. We circled the target three times-- ten minutes to each circle. The tension grew to pure nervousness. Where were the enemy pursuit planes? The sky should be full of them by now! We evidently were waiting for a cloud to drift off the target. Finally, Gimble pressed his mike button, and a muffled "Jesus Cheee-rist!" came over the interphone. When we finally made the bomb run and turned for home, we had clocked forty-five minutes circling the target. I felt myself additionally cold with sweat, but no enemy showed up at all. We laid a good pattern on the target. When the Chin Hills came back in view as we let down to 9000 feet, a microphone in one of the other planes clicked on and over the air came "Show Me The Way To Go Home" with merry variations.

On a Monday in November, an Indian boy from Gaya peddled his bicycle into the open space between the two officers' barracks, cautiously dismounted, all the while soberly watching us watch him. He unfastened a small black box from the center of his bicycle, ambled over to a big tree, and squatted down with his back against it and his rump on the ground, in the approved Indian fashion. He looked from one barracks porch to the other. We looked back, waiting for the show or whatever it would be, to start.

Someone from the other side yelled across, "What the hell cooks?"

"Dunno," Ed shouted back. "Mebbe he's gonna climb a rope and disappear."

Henry Root was working on his gasoline pressure lamp-- made in Japan. Every time he lit it at dusk, we took to the woods. He spilled gasoline all over it, and the lamp stood in a large area of fire until its own gas vaporized and the mantle became incandescent. I still don't know why it never explodes first.

"He's gonna pull out a lamp, rub it, and grant you a wish. Start thinkin' of something good," Henry said.

Major Chick Fountain, our squadron commander, didn't like Indians, and he finally strode out to boot the stranger off the premises. There were a few pieces of rough furniture in the yard that hadn't been put in the rooms. When the Indian boy saw Chick approaching, he beamed momentarily as he grabbed an armchair and placed it a few feet from a table. His features had slid back to impassiveness when Chick came near, but I thought his brown eyes might still be smiling as he offered the chair for Chick to sit in. That stumped our champion. He stopped a moment, and then slouched into the proffered seat with the remark, "Well, let's see what happens, and maybe I'll have a better excuse for throwing him out."

The boy opened his black box, took out two small clay cups, and hurried to the rear of one of the barracks. Gimble had seen some white letters flash on the side of the box, and strolled out to have a look. The boy came scurrying back trying not to spill the dab of water out of the cups. Gimble bent back and roared laughter at the treetops.

"Chick! You're about to get trimmed! This guy is a tonsorial maniac. Look! He held up the little black box to show us the lettering. I read "B-A-R-B-A-R". The boy went to work with the scrutiny of a jeweler, and the haircut wasn't bad. When it came to shaving, he moistened two fingers. Dabbed them on Chick's cheek, and went to work with a dry razor. With a howl, Chick got himself from under the operation, and paid the "barbar" four annas ($8) for the haircut. The shave he would suffer himself to do. The barber thereafter became a daily sight and enjoyed a thriving business, with his cleanliness closely checked by Doc Lipton.

In India, one has a "bearer." I wasn't entirely aware of just what a bearer was when this clean-looking Indian approached our verandah. He had good Caucasian features, but was quite black. He came up with what I thought was a shy manner, and pointing at himself, said "I bearer. You want bearer?"

Whatever it was, I didn't want any, but Jim had heard about bearers and asked how much.

"Twelve rupee."

"A week or a month?" I asked.

"A week, sahib/"

We didn't know then that the English bearers get about thirty rupees a month for running a household from daylight until last tea or drinks at about 10:00 or11:00 P.M. The four of us talked it over and decided we'd let him work for all four.

"He doesn't think he's gonna dress us, too, does he?" Gimble asked.

"I guess we can straighten him out on that point," I said.

The boy's name was Adbul Scoru, but he soon was just "Joe". He came before seven o'clock to shine our shoes, heat water for us to wash in, and do anything else we wanted. We didn't have him make tea, because it was nice to doze to the last minutes, and then wash, dress, and hustle to the mess hall just before it closed at eight. It was no use sleeping through breakfast, because promptly after breakfast, Joe started sweeping and dusting. If you shouted at him to stop, he would either look terribly hurt, or disappear and not clean at all that day. A real Hindu bearer will not sweep the floor. That is the sweeper's job -- a lower caste. The Moslems imitate this to a certain extent, but the fact that Joe would sweep, made us think he might be a coolie getting ahead in the world. We didn't like the idea of being taken in, but, after all, we were supposed to be democratic. Sweeping is done with a bundle of stalks ties together. They stir up the dirt, but don't really remove it.

When Joe applied for employment, he exhausted his knowledge of the English language. We had to use sign language, demonstrate, or make sounds guided by a Hindustani vocabulary. One day, Joe brought us two rice-flour cakes each, in appreciation we thought. They were good. We thanked him. While we were entertaining ourselves with thoughts of what a good man we had, he pointedly mentioned that they cost two annas each. We could have bought all of them for about three annas, but we paid up.

Gaya, politically, is a Congress city, a place easily inflamed against the British by the words of Gandhi, and is totally different from the larger towns on the coast and in the mountains, where the touch of the European is more evident.

On the spiderweb of roads leading into the town, dust lies feather-soft and plush-deep. The pad of barefeet or the slow roll of great wheels of ox-drawn cars lifts the dust in small compact clouds. But when a rickety inter-city bus, slouched askew on its springs, honks down the narrow strip of dust-covered asphalt, powdered grit flies fifteen feet in the air, turbulently whirling and all-effacing. The windows of the bus are alive with black heads and arms and white patches of clothing, and its horn sounds for all the world like a Canadian goose. The sweating black driver keeps one hand squeezing the bulb of his horn, and the oxcarts, bicycles, and pedestrians open a lane just ahead of the uncompromising front bumper. The delirious careening bus dashes on, and its wake of whirling dust devours the patient and choking travelers as they are left to grope for the center of the road again.

On the outskirts of the town, there are a few substantial brick homes in careful settings among winding roads. Their spacious yards of green grass and flowerbeds and shrubs are sometimes enclosed in a low brick fence that fails to obstruct the view, for "who goes by" is a large item in a land of leisure. Yet the fences sets the sedate dwelling apart like a sanctuary amid the aimless confusion of wandering Hindus, water buffalo, oxen, semi-wild hogs, and the ever-encrusting hawks and buzzards. These homes of a few English are truly bits of green, fragrant, comfortable England from which the interests of the Empire, whether religious, political, or industrial, are administered.

Nearer the business district, where the buildings huddle close together, there is a large community swimming pool of warm lifeless water. Its surrounding brick wall is discolored with time and the rains, and across from it is the more familiar lilypad-covered pool, surrounded by another low brick wall. This is the public wash place. Women and men squat besides its muddy green water to pound their wet clothes on flat rocks until they are considered clean. In the country villages, this pool is the water supply for drinking and cooking, for bathing, for washing animals, and for cooling the water buffalo -- the beasts that don't perspire.

With a few steps, you plunge into the turmoil and aromas of Kutchery Road! This is the final day of fasting and feasting to the Sun God. For as far as you can see, the narrow street, lined solidly with ramshackle one- and two-story buildings, is a seething unity of human commotion. But before you can turn into the street, you are assailed by a smell! Only by sheer willpower can you hold your withering stomach in place. Look in the road. Look in the gutter. Sniff at the shops. A hand that occasionally sweeps out of the gloomy interior of one of the little stands attracts the eye. The hand disturbs a horde of flies that lift momentarily from the nuts, cookies, and sticky sweets on the small counter. To another stand two goats are tethered.

From the food, from the goats, from the gutter, the smells come, but part of it you never locate. Sometimes the smell is strong unto nausea. Sometimes it is overridden by the sharp smell of leather. (Leather shops are always run by Chinese. For Hindus consider leatherwork the lowliest of trades.) Sometimes near a small shop will be a deep, sweet, sensual smell of incense.

Now a trio of men with a horn, drums, and cymbal clatters by. The horn is an old valve trombone squawking unceremoniously in the hands of a carelessly turbaned Hindu. The three sound and stumble on, looking back at the Americans. At the sound of a bicycle bell you to turn and move aside. A tricycle'rickshaw, peddled by a coolie fully wrapped in his white sheets, goes past carrying a fat, bewhiskered, high-caste Indian in European clothes, who turns an expressionless face to stare at you. A runner, in a brief loincloth, follows with his loaded'rickshaw in the wake of the tricycle. Now you step back toward the asphalt road to avoid a stern image of Gunga Din, staggering along under the weight of two huge jars of water strung to the ends of a pole bent across both shoulders. He is dressed in a loin winding, and another winding, meant for his chest, is draped about his neck. His hair is so short, that his head looks nearly bald, except for a queue tassel of eight or ten three-inch-long hairs. Following him, is a smooth-featured young wife, carrying a minute chocolate-brown baby snuggled against the orange cloth of her right arm. Her orange "sari", as is the Indian style, hoods her head and swathes her body. The left side of her aquiline nose bears a small silver ornament, and, on her proudly held head, a moderately-filled basket of food, trinkets, or households possessions -- obscure under a dirty cloth -- rides gracefully as her hips absorb the movement of her barefooted strides.

There is a starved beggar, his grey-tinged black hair in wild disorder overhead and face. His brown skin is gray with ashes, and his hips are covered by the windings of a ragged cloth that cannot remember that it was once white. Another long and torn cloth drapes one shoulder like a Mexican serape. When he sleeps by day, it keeps off the flies. By night, it is an attempt at more warmth. These beggars are not yet as aggressive as in westernized India, where tenacity brings wealth from the Europeans. Here, only the children follow you, chanting "No mamma, no papa, no place to sleep, bahksheesh, Bahib!"

Another beggar wanders along apathetically, peering up at shopkeepers piteously, raising a cupped hand, and murmuring some Hindustani phrase as he signals toward his mouth. If someone stops to toss him a coin, it will probably be not more than a twelfth of an anna or a sixth of a cent. Usually a wave of the hand sends him on as the shopkeeper gurglingly spits a red splotch of betelwood juice from his stained teeth and lips into the dust of the road. (Betelnut contains quinine and is used as commonly as gum to help control malaria)

The shops are small open-fronted dens lined solidly side by side on both edges of Kutchery Road. Two worn stones lift you from the street to the shop level, where it is customary to remove your shoes before entering off the narrow approach. Usually Europeans are not required to do this, however.

The dress of the moving multitude is everything from the nakedness of the small children -- their sexes and bulging bellies obvious -- to the men's clothes which may consist of a fancy striped-silk shirt minus the detachable color, worn outside a pair of loose pajama pants. A skirt, made by winding a ten-foot length of cotton cloth at the waist so that it cloaks the body from the waist to the ankles, often replaced the pants. The end of the cloth is lumped under the top, and gives the appearance of a pot belly. Footwear is scarce, but may be anything from a homemade sandal to castoff shoes with the heel cut away to make slippers, or just stamped down and tied onto the foot.

If anything wraps their heads in addition to dust and black hair, it most often is the dirty piece of cloth that might also be wrapped around their chests if the flies or weather make the change advisable. A headdress seen frequently in this Congress town is a politically significant boat-shaped little cotton hat with stiffly starched sides, either white or with a design in color. There are a few tarbooshes. The cloth saris, whose one length wraps the head, body and legs of the woman, are often bright red, or some brilliant solid color, among the poorer people. The wealthier women have beautiful ones of printed or ornamented silk, so sheer that other clothes must be worn beneath them.

Everyone watches the Americans curiously, and I suddenly became aware of the stare of a withered little woman with long saber teeth protruding over her lower lip. As I looked down from her quiet stare, she hobbled away, the big toe of her left foot sticking out at right angles, and her hands clasped behind her bent back to ease the weight of her shoulders. I felt a momentary twinge of unreality, as though I had been thrust into a prehistoric setting. I considered that I had seen a human being linked centuries closer to the animals.

Amid these generally gloomy shops that offered nothing for sale that I could recognize as desirable, there suddenly was a brilliant spot of burnished brass-wares that drew me, because it was more familiar and clean than anything else. A meandering ox changed the flow of people past the shop. An alert and impatient nanny goat darted through the opening first, and I followed. Here was every possible shape of brass that I could dream of, but nothing that was obviously an ashtray, which I could use. The squatting proprietor looked at me from between his knees and made no move to sell. He waited for me to show interest and make an offer.

But before I could decide what I wanted, there was an accelerated movement in the street. Four men, naked to the waist, staggered along with short, quick steps almost at a trot, bearing a draped palanquin hanging from a heavy pole between them. The partially covered feet of a corpse showed at the open front end. A moment later four more men trotted along carrying a covered body on a littler. I found out that all day every day they go by like this taking the dead to the river bank to be burned or just thrown in. The vultures also help in transmuting the flesh to dust, particularly in Benares where there is the Tower of Silence. On a grating in the tower the bodies are laid so the vultures can remove the flesh and let the bones drop through the grating.

In a booth next to the brass store were large sticky-sweet looking black mounds. The sign above the opening said "tobacco". A man brought another mound from the back of the shop, plopped in on the floor, and started mixing it with his hands. The smell was of heavy, sweet, moist tobacco. As I turned to go, the man arced a brilliant wad of betelnut juice over the mound and into the street. It didn't all reach the street. Everywhere the roadway was splotched with these red stains.

Many of the shops have nothing to offer but rusty nuts and bolts in dull brass bowls, or dirty cards of buttons, used-looking razor blades, chains, steel pens, calendars, cheap purses, shoestrings, or spare parts of old flashlights. It looks like a fire sale after a dime store catastrophe. There are booths with stacks of native leaf-wrapped cigarettes and small cardboard packs of English cigarettes. The more prosperous shops sell cotton cloth goods, and here I picked up sheets and a pillowcase for my bed. In another store were a few items of canned food, and as I passed by, Swetland and Gimble came out triumphantly laden with tins of English cookies. I forget just what they paid per box -- two dollars, perhaps. If so, the next time they bought cookies, they cost two and a half.

Ever since one of our enlisted soldiers was nearly killed when he got drunk and tried to break up a native wedding, we could only be in town in the daytime with an M.P. Taylor was an M.P. one night, and as such, he had to raid the forbidden spots -- the brothels and native drinking houses -- with the British police.

Taylor was a hardy little character, but he admitted feeling weak and sick at the stomach from what he had seen.

"No sir, Lt. Gilbert", he said, shaking his head. "I never seen anything like it! I've been in the worst joints in the States and in Panama, but they ain't a candle like this. The stuff these men drink makes 'em crazy, and the women are like animals. I saw one lay her squalling baby over in the corner of the room and take some guy for two annas right there. It makes you ashamed you're a man. That scrawny "madam" or whatever she was, tried to stall us off by saying 'No American now. Before rule, sometime twenty.' We didn't find any of our boys in there."

There was excitement in camp when we returned that day. Some of the soldiers had found and killed a 5' 3" cobra, complete with hood and venom, as opposed to the ones the snake charmers use in the cities. That night there was more excitement. A soldier came into his barracks and approached his bed. In the light of his gasoline lamp, another 5' 3" cobra, the mate of the first, slipped off the bed and glided out the door. The soldier was scared pale. He drew a new cot, blankets, and netting from supply, and moved into another barracks that night.

The weather in November was cool, so that we needed our blankets at night. We went to breakfast wearing jackets, and those who had wool clothes were comfortable, but by mid-morning, those of us who had only cotton were the most comfortable.

Our messing at Gaya was good, but there was too little room at the two tables. The late comers were not always able to dine as well as the first ones, so it was the usual sight to find the officers in pairs drifting around the corner of the barracks a few minutes before chow time. Different pairs would see each other and speed up their walk. It would frequently end in a free-for-all run, with at least two or three men ending up without seats and standing around waiting for someone to finish. Fried chicken became a fairly frequent luxury. The first time it was served, the fact that it was fried in coconut oil made little difference, but when eggs and eggplant and all other fried things tasted of coconut oil, the enthusiasm for fried chicken waned quickly. Doc Lipton, our squadron doctor, finally scurried around and found some cooking oil in Gaya, and only then did fried chicken and eggs and eggplant taste right. The vegetable at Gaya was cauliflower. Day after day after day -- cauliflower.

It was Doc, in addition to his duties of holding a daily sick call, who saw that our water supply was properly chlorinated Water was pumped by coolies into a cement reservoir supported twelve feet off the ground. Here it was chlorinated and then piped to the kitchen and latrines.

Doc also had to superintend the disposal of the garbage. He invited me to go along on the garbage truck one day, saying he had a sight for me to see. I assured him it was purely his overwhelming personality that overrode my distaste for his cargo, and I hopped in the front seat with him and the driver. Two more men went along in the back of the truck. I didn't know why until we reached the dumping area on the far side of town. There were about twenty people there, all with clothes ragged and black. The men were so thin that almost all their bones could be counted, and they were but a degree removed from being naked. The two men in the back of our truck had to shout at the people to kept them away while the barrels of waste were poured to the earth with a nauseating slopping sound. Like a pack of wolves that could not longer be held back, they scrambled on hands and knees in the stuff trying to sort out bones and pieces of scrap meat.

Two children found the largest bone with a little meat on it, but a man immediately snatched it out of their hands and kept it. Empty tin cans ranked with the meat in importance.

On all side were scabby, filthy dogs that trembled at the smell of food, but feared to trespass until the people finished. With the dogs were the ever-present wild-looking pigs, and, flapping their wings in mid-air overhead, were fifty hawks, while perched on nearby trees were about ten big vultures with black and white bodies and red heads.

The men and women and children were gathering morsels from the mess and putting them in their tin cans. One man found a lump of something, shook off stuff adhering to it, and plopped it into his mouth unconcerned. The smell and sight nauseated me so that I had to walk down the road where the truck could pick me up, for fear of adding my own contribution to the scene.

High in India's skies soar the vultures -- the winged scavengers that remove dead infected flesh. From altitudes of five to eight thousand feet, these giant birds with ten food wingspread float lazily on the up currents, never flapping a wing -- just drifting. With keenly detecting eyes, they watch for fighting animals, or grotesquely stiff, dead ones -- usually dogs -- and when a suggestion of a meal exposes itself to view, they fold their wings and plummet to a focal point from scattered areas of sky like stones sliding down the sides of a funnel. They extended their wings in time to break their fall, and in a few minutes, fifteen or twenty great vultures are raucously tearing the dog to pieces. Two or three at a time, they insert their sharply hooked beaks and long necks into the dog's bowels and jerk the carcass back and forth between them. In an hour there is scarcely even skin left on the skeleton. Sometimes the birds fight among themselves, with bodies tilted forward, ugly screaming heads lowered halfway to the ground on their long neck, and wings flapping powerfully, they rush at each other a few times and then one, apparently out-screamed, allows the other to eat alone. They are somber birds. The lines of their folded wings, as they sit by the dead, suggest gravediggers in swallowtail coats, but the red-purple of their heads colors the picture more truthfully.

As scavengers, there was a multitude of brown hawks, which appeared particularly after mess. For a time, when the enlisted men sat in the shade of buildings to eat, the hawks would hover and swoop in endless confusion just overhead, dropping daringly to snatch food from open mess kits or to catch thrown morsels in mid-air.

At night, the screams of a dozen jackals sounded like hundreds of wailing agonized puppies. At dusk the furry canines crept from hiding. All night long the sound of their packs came dimly from the distance, their weird screams reached a crescendo as they passed through the camp and then dwindled away again. Sometimes a single animal crept into an open room, but at any faint sound would slink out again. They never attacked humans. Compared with the frail, starved, scabby domestic dogs that snarled viciously at each other and avoided fights because of their weakness, the fluffy fur of these jackals made them look plump and healthy.

On November 25th, the day before Thanksgiving, we were assembled for an important briefing. The target was to be Bangkok in Indo-China -- about 1000 miles more for the round trip than our then longest run to Rangoon. Nine ships would go, starting at 6:00 P.M., the squadron C.O. first, then our crew. We were to take off three minutes apart and fly at 165 miles an hour at 8000 feet until time to climb to 20,000 feet, In order not to be intercepted by enemy pursuit at Rangoon, and to avoid detection, we would go south of the Rangoon area and cross the Malay peninsula at Tavoy Island. Halfway between the mouth of the river and Bangkok was a particular bend in the river that located the area of an important refinery. In our bomb load were two 1000-pound bombs and a cluster of incendiaries. The fires should be tremendous, and, in spite of the long flight to look forward to, we considered that a good fire which could be seen for a hundred miles or more would make a wonderful sight for us, as well as a good punch for the newspapers.

Taking off a three minute intervals puts the planes a long distance apart -- between eight and ten miles. It is almost impossible to fly B-24s in a night formation for any length of time, because the long wings keep the planes apart and a pilot's eyes tire quickly with the strain of focusing on the dim blue lights of the ship he flies with. He has to stay as close as possible to see the light and then becomes unsure just how far away it really is. Besides, the tactical advantage of a night formation at that time was doubtful. If there were night fighters, they would probably find the bombers first. Bombers are located by the flame and red color at the end of the exhaust where the turbo supercharger is. That was another good reason why we went singly. Four such lights was the smallest number we could have.

It was dark when we took off. The plane carried a tremendous load of gas and bombs, and used all the runway. We had only been out over the water about an hour, when we could see red tracers in the darkness up ahead. Ed and I simultaneously pressed our mike buttons to warn the crew -- and then we looked at each other in the dim cockpit and laughed. It was Fountain's crew ahead testing their guns.

The hours dawdled by while the motors droned in smooth harmony. The seat grew hard. We flew on the auto-pilot and used the lowest power settings that would give us 160 miles and hour. By keeping your men forward in the plane and being sensitive to the feel of the elevator controls, you can increase the air speed without changing the power settings. This is called "having the ship on its step" and corresponds to the step built into watercraft to reduce the drag.

I took a lot of power to maintain speed at first, and the high gas consumption worried us a bit, but we knew it would decrease. At two-hour intervals, to start with, we could make small reductions. The phosphorescent green of the dials stood out of the black instrument panel like ghostwriting. We had coffee, and I sipped it occasionally for something to do. Ed may have dozed. It was hard to tell, the way he hunched himself up on his arm rests and seldom moved.

We knew the moon was due to rise at about ten o'clock, so I was looking for that first sign of pale blue to appear on the black horizon. Then the red lip of the moon itself followed. Whether we were back in the States in bed, or here over the Bay of Bengal, it would rise red and pale quickly as it ascended.

Adam had switched to our second bomb bay tank quite a while before. It was about empty when Swetland called up at eleven thirty to say it was time to run for Tavoy Island, and to give us the next heading. Gimble was dozing on the flight deck behind us, so I had Adam tell him it was time to go into the nose. We were about to start the climb to altitude, and, when we went on oxygen, he would have to stay in one place where his hose connection was.

The change in the roar of the engines as we put on power for the climb brought the whole crew out of their lethargy to put on their masks. A little before one o'clock, Swetland called up to say we were over our checkpoint of Tavoy Island. We were at 20,000 feet and sitting on the edge of our seats looking out. We could barely make out the contour of the hills of Malay in the bright moonlight. Down below, there was quite a bit of haze and a few thin clouds. I had a glimpse of water again and knew we were over the Gulf of Siam. Swetland said it was time to turn. He wanted to get a little closer to shore so he wouldn't miss the mouth of the river. Ed flipped off the auto-pilot switch and flew manually. He looked out the window, then at his instruments. I couldn't see a thing on my side except for an occasional gleam of moonlight on water through holes in the clouds.

We found the mouth of the river easily and turned north. The clouds thinned, and I could see part of the big loop in the river sticking out from under the nose of the plane. I knew Ed could see the sharp bend where the target was. I lifted out of my seat to look out on his side. The bend in the river was clear, but the target area was absolutely black. The bomb doors rumbled open. I looked out for night fighters, but all I could see were about twenty wildly waving searchlights around Bangkok. They didn't reach to half our altitude.

When the bomb release lights flashed, we went into a diving turn. I waited for a report of the fires, and finally called Gimble to ask.

"I saw the flash of the bombs all right," he answered, "but there's not one damn flame. Those were good hits, if I do say so myself."

The time was ten minutes of two.

I was more than a little disappointed about not starting a fire. Maybe we had gotten the wrong bend in the river, but there was nothing to do now but head home. Right away, as we descended to 9,000 feet, we cut the r.p.m.s and manifold pressure back. We had been running on the wing tanks for about four hours, and they would have to last eight hours more. We are used to talking about "sweating" over enough gas to last a moderately driven car about two years.

The trip home was absolutely the longest drag I have ever calloused my posterior over. I got up once or twice, but I didn't like to leave the cockpit with the autopilot on and Ed apt to doze. An airplane is something that can't be left alone for a minute with safety. As the gas load became lighter, we cut back more power and maintained about 160 miles an hour.

At dawn, we were still nearer to Burma than India. Everyone but Ed, Swetland, and I were sound asleep. I was keeping a tabulation of the gas gauge readings so we could tell our consumption and estimate how long we could fly. At that time I figured there would be about enough gas to fill my cigarette lighter by the time we reached Gaya -- I hoped we could make Calcutta. But the consumption grew less with time.

The drone of the motors had a beautiful sound. If one so much as missed a beat, everyone on the plane would be on their feet fastening parachutes.

We reached the coast at 7:45 A.M. and figured we could reach home all right. Then we cut the power a little more. We finally landed at Gaya at five minutes of ten -- it lacked five minutes of being sixteen hours. As tired as we were, we were wreathed in smiles because the thing was over. For a while we didn't much care whether we'd bombed anything or not. It was just good to be home. As we taxied to our parking place, the engines -- all four of the beautiful things -- sounded throaty and confident and unemotional. Given gas and oil, they would start out again right now. I went mortally numb at the thought and turned my mind to the bed that awaited with open covers. We had less than 100 gallons per engine left, but it was still a safe margin.

After interrogation, there was a big turkey feast waiting for us.

"That's right," I remembered, "it is Thanksgiving!"

For a multitude of little things I was thankful. Before I could think further, I was asleep.

The last thing I did before leaving Gaya for our new base near Calcutta, was to see the famous Buddha-Gaya Temple, three miles away on the bank of a river. The story I gathered from one of the priests is that the original was destroyed or decayed ages ago, and that this new one was built in its place 200 years B.C. There must have been a lull in Buddhism at some time, because this temple became partially buried and was unearthed in 1880. It is over 150 feet high, built like an elongated pyramid of stone and brick, black with age. It certainly was no gleaming thing of the mysterious East. There was one small room where the main Buddha was, and it was the only figure still showing signs of being washed with gold. A length of cloth was hung from its neck to clothe its body. The facial features were full and showed no definite character. There were offerings of flowers in the Buddha's hand, and an intelligent-looking priest was taking his turn squatting on the worn stone alter acting as intermediary for the gifts of flowers and little oil lamps that devotees desire placed before the Buddha. The altar room was small, bare, and dank. With an attitude of great reverence I was shown a green scummy pool in which the Great Buddha was wont to bathe. I believe they consider the scum as a lovely green blanket.

The burial places of the priests are scattered about the bare sunken yard. Some of the circular monuments have as many as 400 Buddhas carved on them. There are numerous stone carvings from the old temple leaning against trees in the yard, and at the back of the temple is a Buddha sitting in the customary position with crossed feet. Before him is the stone upon which Prince Gautama sat under the Bo tree when he received the divine inspiration. It was difficult for me to view this place religiously when the priests seemed so unconcerned. Yet Buddha has more followers than any other religion in the world.

From the point of view of us "wolves" the best part of the whole trip to the temple was the sight of a lovely Burmese girl who had made a pilgrimage there. She had a beautifully coiffured mass of black hair, smooth tanned features, and was otherwise quite divinely designed, we thought. That was a breathe of fresh air.

That night we heard the Jap radio that called itself the "Voice of Malacca," to sound like the authentic "Voice of Calcutta," report that three British planes dropped incendiaries over Bangkok. "They are believed to be based in China, since any other bases are 3000 miles away." The fact that they didn't mention the refinery might have indicated that we did do some damage after all. It wasn't long before our command received a hot letter from General Chennault requesting that we limit ourselves to Burma -- the Japs were retaliating against him. However, the enemy soon found out from their estimated 500 spies in the Calcutta area that the bombers were based at Gaya and they devoted a special broadcast to threats of wiping us out. One of their long distance reconnaissance planes did come over the field at about 30,000 feet or more. The sound of its motor was barely discernable in absolute stillness and the plane, when finally spotted, looked like a moving speck of the sky itself. In addition to the difficulty of getting bombers that far into India, we doubted if they would bomb the center of Buddhism. Their bombers never came.

Chapter VI

OPERATIONS FROM PANDA

Our new base was about a hundred miles from Calcutta. There were a few permanent brick buildings that had been part of the colliery. One new barracks, similar to the ones at Gaya, had been built, another was under construction, and two more were planned. Evidently we were to expand!

Joe, our bearer, followed us to Panda but grew slovenly and occasionally disappeared in the afternoon. We cut his pay to eight rupees one week, and immediately had the best bearer in camp. I believe Joe got both wealthy and homesick. He asked for a leave to go back to Gaya, and found someone named Mohammed Haneef to replace himself. Joe never returned, and the replacement soon became head bearer. He was wonderful. He was from Simla in the north and much more energetic than the Bengalese. In addition, he could speak good English and became general interpreter for the whole camp. He was lean and hard, and had an ugly scar at the outer corner of his left eye, but we grew to have almost utter faith in his acts and suggestions. I say almost because of a story we heard about an excellent bearer that had served an American faithfully for ten years. He could be trusted absolutely with money and had plenty of opportunities to steal. However, when it came time for his master to leave for the United States, he was told to pack the trunks and bags as he had done before. The American himself packed the bag he was to take in his hand on the train and boat. When he arrived in the States and opened his other bags, all he found were stones and dirt. Everything else had been taken.

Our bearers kept our rooms and clothes straightened, sewed buttons on, prepared buckets of hot and cold water in the little booth on the back porch where we took baths, brought cold drinks and ice cream from the bar -- when we had either -- and sometimes fixed tea. At first it made me self-conscience to be called "Master", but I eventually was able to order Mohammed about as he expected a master to do.

The targets we went after from the new base were the same as before. There were still only two squadrons of us. One had remained at Gaya until its new base could be finished. So far, out of about a dozen missions we had lost only one crew whose plane had been damaged from ack-ack over Rangoon. And that crew was from the other squadron.

One of the targets that was causing us trouble was Mytinge Bridge. It was a narrow-gauge railway bridge about twenty miles south of Mandalay. I doubt if it was more than six feet wide. Our heavies didn't dare go below 16,000 feet to bomb because of the ack-ack concentrations. The big mistake we made was in not going in low to knock it out the first time. That one time there had been no guns. The next day we went back and met the heaviest gun concentration in Burma. The Japs had moved it in overnight. Time and time again a formation of six or nine planes dropped their twenty or so bombs on the bridge. The target would disappear in mushrooms of dust and water, but it was not destroyed. An approach might be damaged -- the wooden piers might need repair, but the bridge still stood. Nearby paddy fields remained well ploughed by our bombs. The B-25's went against the bridge too, But with about the same luck. All we were doing was slowing traffic and not much more.

The Colonel decided we were wasting a lot of time and money, so he decided to make a low-level attack himself in a B-17. We had three sad-looking B-17s at the field that remained from the year before. They had no superchargers and could not go to high altitudes. The Colonel and a Major, who was to be C.O. of a newly formed squadron at our field, were to go in at fifty feet and hit the bridge immediately after a formation of B-24s bombed from the regular altitude. After we bombed, we made a big circle and strained our eyes on the bridge. No B-17 appeared. We circled again and finally headed home. Fully an hour after we landed, the 17s limped home, each with a motor feathered and riddles with small caliber holes. Two mighty disheartened crews stepped out. It had been a flight for the books all right, but one little thing had gone wrong. The navigator had missed a checkpoint that whizzed past him, and they followed the wrong road to the target. A bridge near a bend of a river loomed up about when it should have. At that speed and low angle, everything looked all right, but as the bombardiers released the bombs they saw that the bridge already had its center span out. It was another bridge on another river that had already been destroyed. As they flew over the Burma countryside, the people did everything but throw rocks at the planes. Pistols and rifles and light guns were the only things that could move fast enough to be fired at them, but in spite of the large number of holes, the worst wounds among the crew members were scratches made by flying bits of aluminum. The one twenty millimeter shell that hit the Colonel's ship would have gone through the head of his bombardier had he not just that instant leaned forward to look into his bombsight. The shell passed through the ship without exploding.

In January and February of 1943, our group began to be more than just a couple of squadrons, and we changed from makeshift to organized operation. The other two squadrons of the Group were formed and new crews came in. Ed, who had been the Intelligence Officer, was made Operations Officer. We received an Intelligence Officer especially trained for the job and he gathered all the information there was about Burma. He posted what he could in an attractive form so that the crews would learn more about current numbers and types of enemy pursuit that were based near our targets. For each crew member, he made emergency kits containing a silk map of Burma, a compass, a blood chit similar to the one we used in the desert, string and fish hooks, iodine for purifying water, and elements of a first aid kit. He also obtained a large number of silver rupee pieces and had canvas belts made to hold them. They were to be used to buy our way out of Burma if, we were captured by the Burmese. The belt was a heavy thing to wear, but there was no doubt of its value. Only a few of the Burmese were sympathetic to the Allies. Most of them would probably turn white men over to the Japs, and there were parts of northwest Burma where the native might even kill us of their own choice. While the desert had offered a good chance for lost crews to return, the outlook for anyone forced down in Burma was definitely bleak. Men just weren't coming back. Even if they could get to the Chin Hills, they stood the chance of getting lost in the jungles, starving, being too wounded to walk out, becoming weak from malaria or other fevers, contracting sickness from bad water, or running into head hunters, some of whom still practiced their charming customs. The danger from wild animals was not great.

There weren't many answers to being forced down at sea near enemy territory. If the plane stayed in one piece, if the dinghies released from their racks, if the men could get out of the plane into the water, and get into the dinghies, they still didn't have much of a chance. We maintained a sea patrol boat, but it couldn't go as far as we did without being a dead pigeon for the enemy. The one real chance was that the emergency radio in the dinghy would send out a signal that a flying boat could pick up and use to locate the survivors. The only answer was not to be shot down. So far we had been lucky. We had lost only two crews, but one ship out of a formation was sixteen percent, far greater than was being lost in other theaters.

The press correspondents, Walter Briggs and Toby Wiant flew with us on several missions over Rangoon. On the first one we did not see a single pursuit, and the ack-ack was scattered and ineffective in comparison with what the Germans offered. Briggs was along on the second mission and he saw what he was after. As we bombed and turned from the target, the gunners reported enemy pursuit taking off from

Mingladon airport across the river from the town. Within a few minutes we saw three Zeros climbing up on our right. They seemed to be coming up at fifty-degree angle, fairly hanging on their propellers, and they leveled off 3,000 feet above and ahead of us. One turned back toward us and did two beautiful slow rolls.

"They stunt like Italians," I thought. The Italians were noted for the way they did acrobatics just out of range of our guns, and then went back to their airfields without making a pass. On the third slow roll, the Jap stayed on his back and dove straight at us upside-down. We could see the flame from his guns, and he kept coming. Our tracer bullets went toward him, but were wild as he came close to the formation and dove below. The next Jap was directly above and dove straight down through the center of our element with his guns spurting red, but hurting no one. For the first time I saw the man and not merely his silhouette inside an enemy plane, but it was a lightning glimpse that offered no detail. The plane was unpainted aluminum with a big red circle on each wing.

Then came the most outstanding attack I have ever seen. The third pursuit was well above and slightly ahead of the formation. He rolled on his back and dove at the wing ship across from me -- Henry Root's. Henry said afterward he knew that plane was out to ram him, and he was getting ready to slip to one side. The Jap reached our altitude not more than 200 feet behind the tail of Henry's ship, still diving slightly on his back, Executing a pullout that seemed impossible for both machine and pilot, he pulled his nose down and up through 110 degrees of arc so that his wing guns were practically muzzle to muzzle with the tail turret guns of Henry's ship. Both sets of guns blazed in rapid fire for what must have been no more than three seconds, although it felt like fifteen minutes while the pursuit hung in mid-air. Then it flipped over on its back and dived away apparently unhurt. There was not a single scratch on the B-24 because the wing guns of the enemy were spread far enough apart that the fuselage of the bomber fitted in part of the dead area between the parallel paths of fire. How the tail gunner could have missed the pursuit, I have no idea.

One of our regular missions was to patrol the Japanese sea-lanes from the Andaman Islands to below Tavoy Island. We usually cruised in formation at no less than 10,000 feet to stay out of the effective range of a cargo vessel's guns. If there were escorting ships, as there seldom were, we had to go higher before attacking. Sometimes when the sea haze was particularly bad, we would spread the formation out wing abreast about five miles apart where one plane could just see one other on each side. In this manner we flew down one strip of sea-lane and up another.

On one occasion a large vessel that appeared to be a troop carrier was sighted. Number two plane reported it and the rest of us assembled in formation within sight of the ship and began to climb to 14,000 feet, just to be on the safe side. It was a formidable-looking target. The lead plane was Ed's and he brought the flight over on a bomb run. A limited amount of ack-ack was bursting fairly near us as the bombs were released. There were no direct hits by five of the planes, although damage was done by two near misses. The leader of the second element, Sloan, was bound that such a luscious target should not get away, so he left the formation and went down to 6000 feet to release his bombs. There had been some malfunction in his bomb release mechanism on his first run. The ack-ack from the ship had stopped and small motor launches were pulling away. Mike Simmons, Sloan's bombardier, made a prefect run and released his eight 500 pounders. At the moment of impact, a waist gunner back by the camera hatch snapped one of the best bomb hit pictures the War Department has. All bombs hit on the rear half of the target with a terrific flash and seemed to break the ship in two. Only because we were low on gas did we refrain from going to strafe.

There is an interesting part of aerial warfare that was very hush-hush until the outcome of this war was virtually assured, and even now it cannot be told. This is aerial mining. The British have admitted that their island was virtually out of the war even before Dunkirk because of the extent to which the Germans had mined the harbors by aerial methods. Mines are particularly deadly because none of their blast effect is expended on the open air. Even though a mine explodes 100 feet under a ship, the water transmits the blast almost undiminished to the bottom of the vessel and may break its back. In the case of heavily armored vessels, the underside is the only vulnerable point.

Mines can be equipped with timing devices to counteract attempts to sweep them. At one time, enemy submarines were leaving their pens in the wake of a minesweeper. The sweeper exploded the mines that were ready to explode and the submarine left before other mines became armed. To counteract this, a mine was devised to explode on the second impulse -- that of the submarine. It blew the submarine out of the water a few hundred feet behind the sweeper.

The possibilities of mine-laying are unending. It was mines and not bombs that broke the great Mohne Dam in Germany. A mine does not actually have to explode to do the enemy damage. If he knows the mine is in his channel, he will keep important traffic cut until satisfied the danger is over. Mining tends to be a secret business, however, because a sunken vessel most effectively blocks a channel, and the vessel will cooperate only if the presence of the mine is not known. If a target area becomes too tough for a formation to tackle in daylight, a point in the channel removed from the guns may be mined at night.

Another advantage of mining is that it can be used in bad weather, at low altitudes, in poor visibility, and by single ships when a formation could not successfully bomb. There are times when the weather over the Bay of Bengal is just plain dirty. There is no real character to it. The sky is littered with clouds -- soft little puffs, giant bulging white ones, thin lifeless layers, or a forbidding tangle of many black ones. As far as can be seen, there is this pointless variety. Sometimes they envelope a formation unexpectedly and make the planes scatter so that a bombing mission is abortive. When weather like this is present, mining can still be done.

As far as we knew, our Group was the first of Americans to do aerial mining. The British did the briefing. It was long and technical and detailed. Eight ships took off at 9:00 A.M. to mine the mouth of the Irrawaddy below Rangoon. They flew about five minutes apart at an altitude of 500 feet to avoid any chance of detection. It meant flying on instruments only 500 feet above the Bay of Bengal for four or five hours, and doing very excellent navigation to find a precise point from which to orient the mine pattern in the dark. It meant strained eyes and Longine timing to convert airspeed and time to the distance between mines in the limited space of an unseen channel. For precision work, mining ranks with the very finest bombing. One pilot, while flying to his pin point from which his bombardier would time the releases, heard a waist gunner report the presence of night fighters -- he could see their exhaust flames. The pilot ordered his gunners to hold fire until they were fired on. In a few seconds, the four exhaust flames, not of enemy pursuit but of another B-24, passed close above them.

The men who mined were told very little about what they were actually doing. It was secret. At first they became disgruntled about the effort expended and the lack of visible results. The future attitude toward good mining was assured, however, about two weeks later when we were on another "milk run" mission to Rangoon and saw the superstructure of a submerged vessel in the river channel. From the then on, we were interested in mining.

About that time, we also received a report out of Indio-China that the refineries at Bangkok had been well knocked out for an indefinite period. At the time we had bombed, the refinery was operating, although thoroughly blacked out. Important lines, distilling, and power units had been destroyed. That was good, but we still cursed the incendiaries that failed to illuminate our work of art with the flame it deserved.

On January 8th, seven planes went on an armed reconnaissance. We went out to look over the enemy, but we were loaded with bombs and ammunition. First we circled the Andaman Islands to check on shipping and new installations, then inspected its main harbor of Port Blair, flew across the Gulf of Martaban to Moulmein, and having found nothing decided to leave our bombs on the docks so as to lighten the plane for the long voyage home. As the British would say, it was a "poor show". Something went wrong, and the bombs fell on part of the town. We felt pretty bad about traveling so far to kill civilians.

We had wasted too much time in our travels, and on the way home were confronted with the problem of using more gas to reach home sooner -- and possibly running out of gas before we got there -- or cruising as we should and having to find our field in the dark. The countryside tends to be a polka-dot field of dim lights at night, and the haze obscures the distinguishing features such as rivers, and railroads. We decided to take a chance on the dark, and were within fifty miles of the field when the last faint after-lightness of duck left us alone above the maze of pinpoint lights. The formation had broken up earlier.

Adamowski and I kept checking the gas until it got so low I was afraid to be out of my seat in case we suddenly had to make a forced landing in the dark or warn the crew to bail out. When I figured that we had about twenty minutes of gas left, we began to gain altitude to bail out. Swetland had gotten what he thought was a definite "fix" just before dark, and he gave us a heading that should have brought us out over the field. We found out later that we could not have missed it by over a half mile.

Ed was about to level off at 5000 feet when I saw that I thought was a red beacon, but as we came near, it turned out to be a big bonfire. Near it, however, were definite bright lights of a landing strip. We didn't know whose, but that didn't matter now. We shot off a double red flare that meant "emergency", let our wheels down and were actually on our approach to the runway when a red flare was shot off from the ground. That meant "don't land".

All we could do was pull up and go around, and shoot off two more red flares. We didn't know whether to bail out while we had time, or stick it out. If the motors were to stop at an altitude of 1000 feet we wouldn't have much chance at night.

On the ground, headlights of a car sped and bounced in irregular paths. The lights on the runway were turned off. From amid the confusion a flashlight blinked "Can you wait five minutes?" Golly, but I was glad I could read code! Chadwick blinked back "No!" And shot off another red flare.

Then I noticed that a straight row of lights was being formed. It seemed to be made of the flickering flare-pots that the British used. After we had slowly circled twice, a green flare arched up from the ground. I have never seen a more delightful sight,

When we were no more than twenty feet above the ground, Ed shouted a "Jesus Kee-rist!" The place where we were to land looked like a grass-grown field with a shallow ditch in it and B-24s need a hard, smooth surface to land on.

We hit he ground and hung on, waiting for the landing gear to give way when it hit the ditch, but our fears petered out when we barely felt the traversing of it.

The field proved to be the one we had heard of called Digri, about eighty miles south of Panda. These men of Digri were of the Wellington squadron we heard had given Burma quite a night pounding recently. No sooner were we parked than lorries arrived to take us to the officers' quarters and mess -- and bar. We found out the reason the first runway lights had been turned off. There was a new runway under construction with three piles of rock and a steamroller. The lights were on so that the natives could see to work. It was a lucky thing for us that their "Duty Officer" was alert.

These Englishmen had formerly been at our base, and had been moved south to make room for us. Each officer took one of the four of us to his room in a bamboo shack in a bamboo thicket. The turbaned bearers brought hot water for us to wash in, and then hastened to the mess hall to prepare our supper. The meal was ready in fifteen minutes, and it was good if not elaborate. We weren't allowed to eat in silence for our hosts gathered in the mess hall with us and kept us engaged in cheerful conversation about ourselves while we ate. After dinner, we adjourned to the bar, a little building made from sheets if bamboo stripping. During the entire evening, we were not allowed to buy a single drink. Our chairs were out in the open as there was no where else to sit. The gin and whisky drinks were warm, partly because the British have no respect for chilled drinks and partly because ice was hard to get.

One of them, a little shyly, made a wonderful crack at us. He said, "You Americans are really unique! When you make a drink, you put sugar to make it sweet, and then lemon to make it sour. You put in gin to make it warm, and ice to make it cold, then you say, 'Here's to you!' and you drink it yourself!' Over a year later, I found the same words in "Reader's Digest".

The Englishmen had a book they called the "Line Book". When an officer, in the course of a story, said what the rest considered to be a "line", it was written in the book and whoever signed it received a free drink on the "Liner".

I've forgotten the officer's name, but I remember that he was a blond good-natured boy who looked like someone I had gone to school with. He seemed to be the slightly cocky kind of capable pilot. I recalled reading in the Calcutta paper a few days before about a Wellington that had limped home from a night raid on Burma, barely able to maintain the height of the valleys in the Chin Hills with its one good motor. On top of that, three Jap pursuits were working him over. He retold the story for us, and then made a mistake,

"Hell! It was a bloody good show, but I wasn't really scared, you know!"

Such a great din of laugher, I have never heard from so few men.

"If I ever heard a line," said the big Squadron Leader with the bushy mustache, "that is it!" With a flourish of pencils, we signed our names and the next round was on the pilot in spite of his failing protests.

I was awakened in the morning by a bearer sneaking my shoes out to be shined, and later by the clatter of chinaware containing my tea. Outside there was hot water for shaving. These English are wonderful hosts! Apparently the difference between British and American hospitality is that the British attend to your food, shelter, equipment, and entertainment, always keeping ahead of your wants, while Americans say to a guest "If there is anything at all I can do for you, just let me know." The Americans eagerly intend every fulfillment of their offer, however.

Next morning we took the Englishmen through our plane. At the sight of the ashtrays, they were most amazed because they never smoke inside a Wellington. The gasoline vapors are always strong.

We flew back to Panda in time for lunch.

Chapter VII

OFF DUTY

Much has been said about the part combat plays in returning men to the religion our elders believe we have turned our backs on. There are many sides to a religious problem, and so I believe the attitude of our bomber squadrons is worth mentioning.

I understand that the chaplains who have been in the front lines with their men have been able effectively to lead them under the terrific stress of front lines warfare, where men are driven through such a hell that they know their own powers are not enough to keep them alive. If a man has been dubious about whether or not the Keeper of the Universe actually listens and heeds the pleas of one of these billions of crawling things on earth, certainly in the midst of shell concussion and flying fragments and land mines is a good place to give those long-neglected prayers a try. At least, it may be the last chance.

If what he desires comes to pass, and it seemed almost impossible, the soldier is convinced that God is truly there and heeding. Finally he has a refuge, and the thought puts his mind at ease. But if what he asks does not come about, his mind must give an answer, and if the problem is too great for the mind, insanity is sometimes the alternate outlet.

But in our war in bombers, we are not subjected to hour after hour after hour of hell, although the men who flew over Fortress Europe certainly approached that condition. In our Eastern Theatre we were not under stress of combat long enough at one stretch when life was rattling out of our control that we had to turn our back on our long reign of self-sufficiency and frantically throw ourselves upon a Higher Care. But the time between one scared spell of combat and the next gave idle days for the mind to reflect on the plan of things.

"If the world works on probability, I wonder if my number is going to come up?"

"I wonder if God knows who's going to die on the next mission?"

"Will it help me to pray even if I don't have utter faith in prayer?"

It takes an able man and a trusted man, whether commanding officer or chaplain, to guide and comfort in those times of quandary.

Our chaplain was not such a man, and I have met a few Protestant ministers who were. The Chaplain was a man in his early fifties whom we had little respect for because we could view him as little else than as unctuous hillbilly. Before coming to us, he had spent many years as a missionary in Africa. I hope he was able to aid the Africans, but he was not young and energetic enough to work with us, and he hadn't enough wisdom and attraction of age to appeal to us. He tried to organize sports, but the young Special Services Officer was much more interested. The only time that the Chaplain came to us was in the mess hall, where we all ran poor seconds to his reach and capacity, and at the bar where he thought he could endear himself to us over convivial wine. The serving blow was his attempt to prefer charges against an enlisted man who, without permission, borrowed his idle staff car to drive five miles to a quarter master supply for needed clothes.

Before our combat became extremely hazardous, the Protestant chapel attendance was small, and in the fall months of 1943, when the casualties in our squadron mounted rapidly, the men who remained said they thought chapel attendance improved slightly. Perhaps the boys found what they were looking for there, but I doubt it. I believe they were trying a last hope.

I know that some will answer this by saying it was unfortunate that we had a poor chaplain. That is true, but it is not the answer. I am now associated with men from every combat air force, and the stories they tell about the inadequate part their chaplains played are almost identical.

I knew another chaplain whom we admired very much for his athletic prowess when we played baseball and volleyball together, but time after time only three men out of 200 odd in the Squadron attended his church services.

Sunday is not a day off in a combat outfit. When part if the day is free, writing letters, reading, "shooting the bull", gambling and drinking still run chapel functions a competitive race. If men are not interested enough to go to a particular building at a particular time to hear and participate in religious programs, then those programs must not have any meaning for the men. Either the chapel building is not considered a sanctuary for the soul, or the men with those souls do not feel in need of such a place. I believe the need is still there, but impassioned recitals and mouthings based on that truly great historic works, the Bible, are no longer considered an adequate answer to men's searching for their God. A search is a moving thing, and our creeds have become stagnant.

I recall two statements made by chaplains, which helped to discredit their positions as leaders. Before I went overseas, many of us read a printed statement in the papers giving an army chaplain's opinion that there was very little drinking in the Army. He could not have known a cross-section of his men or have visited a bar near an army post. On another occasion, a chaplain included this in his payer: "In all our turning unto Thee, we have never turned unto Thee in vain." Even the prayers of non-combat women and children have ended in the gurgle of blood.

Protestant church attendance in the army is not high where the men are away from their womenfolk, as we were. The Catholic boys went by truck to a church in the nearby town of Asansol, and their numbers were consistent and larger than the Protestants. Gimble did not go every Sunday, but being Catholic, he went much more frequently than the other three of us. Twice was too much for Ed and me, and I doubt if Paul went to chapel more than five times.

I don't want to give the impression that the men in my squadron were not religious. We talked about religions and philosophies often, but we considered our opinions less biased than the chaplains'. If religion is a conviction that a particular way of life is best for men to live together in peace and achievement, then those boys were, in good measure, religious.

Although I am not a Catholic or Jew, I admire the way some of their religious men are accepted as "part of the gang", for in that way they are able to achieve the best results. I believe our Protestant ministers are more restricted from drinking, gambling, and smoking, and if they come up to a gathering when either of the first two is going on, they are a definite wet blanket unless they enter in or are known not to disapprove.

The manner in which men lead their lives will be improved in the long run only because they see another way of life that they consider better. The best spiritual leaders in combat were those who were not labeled "spiritual leader". They were the men, among them our commanding officers, who went through the same ordeals that we did, and who, either by will power or conviction, allowed no anxiety to show in their words or acts. They might say, "Sure I was scared, but I guess we just have to put up with it." But the way they would grin it off and go on another mission without a murmur was an example that other men could follow. These men were our real leaders.

We had movies in camp almost every night. They took place outdoors, where a screen made from a sheet was fastened on a framework between two trees. The seats were ordinary wooden benches. Recent pictures from the States were flown to India and made a circuit of all the camps. I believe nothing else did quite so much for moral as the movies did. They brought the tenderness and comedy of home life, thoughts of which had lain dormant in us for months. There was a freshness and reality in what we saw that letters could not bring. What a whistle the San Francisco Bridge or Fifth Avenue or the Statue of Liberty brought forth! I shall never forget the burst of laugher that swept over the audience after two days of gloom followed the death of one of our gunners. The movies had been serious, and then up popped the insolent Bugs Bunny gnawing on a carrot. The crowd came alive. It was good to see them throw their heads back and laugh. The first laugh was such a happy relief that the succeeding waves came with increasing vigor. It was wonderful to behold!

During the intervals between reels, flashlights from various points were shown upward into the night, and when a moth was spotted. All the beams tracked it as though it were an enemy plane. Often the moth went into a spiral and fell out of the lights.

It was in that open-air camp theatre that I found a break in the laces of my emotions. I had never before been deeply stirred by the sentiment in a movie, but suddenly I found myself choking and shuddering with an unwonted sob upon hearing a poignant phrase well spoken, or seeing someone else's deeply moving joy or sorrow. Some part of my emotions which was beyond my control was responding, and though I have been home for a year, this thing still goes on in response to almost anything of that nature which I see or read, and only now do I realize what my subconscious, free from the inhibiting hand of trained reaction, felt then: a deeper understanding of joy and sorrow, derived from its own experiences. I suspect that similar disturbances were taking place within the other men of our camp, but such things were never admitted then.

In our squadron were two enlisted men who had been an announcer and an engineer for a radio station. Noting the lack of music in camp and the fact that the men would rather listen to good American recordings from a Jap radio station than to the limited English language broadcasts from Calcutta, they decided to try something. In the technical supply warehouse building, which was on the airfield, they set up an electric phonograph and a supply of good records. Then one night they called up the operator and said they had an American program directly from the States -- maybe some of the boys would want to hear it. The operator rang the phones where he knew men were on night duty. Over the telephone a dozen men with mouths open and delighted smiles on their faces heard an "American broadcast" -- Tommy Dorsey's orchestra and Bing Crosby as guest singer. But best of all were the commercials. Those silly comments about foods that had made them distinguished back home were wonderful to hear again: "And if you will serve only Canada Dry beverages at your next party, your friends will acclaim you as the toast of the hosts!" Golly! That was really America!

It was nearly two weeks before the hoax was discovered, but it was just as big a hit thereafter. Sometimes English families in nearby communities would call up our operator and ask if the American broadcast were going to be on that night. They heard it regularly over their telephones. When everyone knew who was putting the broadcast on, the boys could color the commercials with remarks like "Hop in the nearest G.I. truck and drive down to the studio. You still have a chance to watch tonight's broadcast."

Judging somewhat from the letters, but mostly from conversation, the headlines from our paper, the C.B.I. (China, Burma, India) Round up, which will be the longest remembered were first of all about the strikes -- those stories aroused tremendous resentment against labor at home. Next in importance was the Errol Flynn case, with such headlines as "All But The Shoes Came Off In Flynn Case". Baseball and the Charlie Chaplin-Joan Barry case tied for third place.

As the months dragged on, the problems of the Squadron Doctor who succeeded Doc Lipton became more taxing. The midsummer heat would knock men over at their work, and only immediate attention would save them from death. Another trouble was that men missed the sexual relations of home, and if they became too drunk or disheartened they sometimes sought what satisfaction they could find. But there was no safe place anywhere. It is true that the black population seemed to grow whiter, as they put it, but the syphilis rate of the natives was nearly 90%. At one time, because of the rising venereal rate, the Doc was kiddingly called a "chancre mechanic". One soldier thought he had a solution, and Doc, at his wit's end to protect his men, decided to "play ball". The soldier obtained a fourteen-year-old girl from a village for a few annas. The girl was quite willing and so were her parents, for a fourteen-year-old is a woman. The Doc examined her and declared her safe. The girl knew what was expected when a soldier gave her some soap and took her to the shower. For half an hour she scrubbed off the filth that she had lived in all her life. The boy finally took her to his room. In ten minutes she came sailing out the door.

"She still stinks," was his only explanation, but I think it went much deeper than that.

The Doctor had trouble more than once with the effects of the local liquor. One afternoon, two G.I.s drank a quantity of Indian rum. Personally, I wouldn't burn the stuff in my lamp. Not long thereafter they were sitting along the side of a railroad embankment where the track ascended a low hill. As an approaching train slowed down on the grade, the two boys jumped into the cab and threw out the wildly screaming Hindu engineer and fireman. The train was a small one of a few cars that were being taken from this branch line onto the main line. All afternoon, the soldiers ran the train as though it were a new toy -- out to the main line, down the switchyards, and bewildered by the maze of tracks and switches, they put it in reverse and went back to the branch line to our field, changing the switches themselves. It was a wonderful afternoon, but it had to end in court-martials.

The Squadron Doc, like many others, had read as a medical student about many skin diseases which were rare in the United States, but were quite common in India, and initially he derived some pleasure from our developing these troubles he hadn't seen before. But in the long run, the skin diseases settled down to ringworm, and several scaly conditions we labeled "Dhobi Itch", because they were supposedly acquired through the native laundrymen who were called "Dhobis". The scale was bothersome and very hard to cure. Under the septic conditions of heat and moisture, "athlete's foot" spread rapidly and several men had to be grounded on that account alone. Of course there were always a little malaria and dysentery.

To us laymen, elephantiasis was a novel and horrible burden for a human being to bear, even though we saw natives daily who had arms or legs swollen with the malady and were trying to continue work. The most pitiful case I saw which may have been a manifestation of elephantiasis was a naked man squatting alone and motionless by the side of a narrow road in a dismal part of Calcutta. His testicles were swollen so that he appeared to have a bulging football between his legs. I did not see him attempt to stand or walk, but unless someone else earned food for him, beggary would be his only alternative.

In this part of India, the soil, where it is not volcanic, is cut into minute paddy fields separated from each other by foot-high ledges. The family fields have been divided between sons until they barely supply the present families with food. In the monsoon season, when rain softens the rock-hard mud, the countryside turns out to plant rice shots, and when the rice matures the villagers again swarm out of their dark, filthy cubicles for the cutting and threshing. In the interests of war the earth of the paddy fields has been dug up for roads and revetments, and rocks from the countryside have been gathered for runways.

On one hot afternoon, when men were digging and women and children were carrying the earth in baskets on their heads, a group of these ragged, dirty coolies gathered to one side of the others. Curiously, I drove my jeep past the. On the hard, dusty surface of the ground lay an Indian woman having her child. The head and shoulders of the shiny, wet little baby were already in the hands of a midwife, so the mother must have been working through part of her labor. A dirty cloth was spread and the baby placed on it with the umbilical cord still intact. Part of the crowd turned back to their digging and carrying. For fifteen minutes, the mother and silently living child lay in the hot sun until the cord dried. Then the mother snapped the cord between her fingers and tied it next to the baby's body. Picking the child up, she carried it fifty feet further from the area of work and put it down again on a cloth, still in the broiling sun that was making the dull metal on my jeep burn through my have khaki trousers. The baby began to squall and I drove away as the mother went back to carrying dirt in her heavy wicker basket. The whole episode had taken no more than forty-five minutes.

On Wednesday, December 23, our crew was given a leave. We threw some clean things in a bag, including a bottle or so of the foul Carew's gin, and the Colonel flew us down to Calcutta, situated on a branch of the Ganges called the "Hooghly". All nine of us took rooms in the swarming Grand Hotel on Chowringhee Road. I imagine that it used to be a fine hotel for tourists, but after the little bombing the city received a week of ten days before, thousands of the native population were leaving on the roads with the wildness of animals leaving a forest fire. This meant that bearers and coolies were leaving jobs, and the service of the hotel suffered.

Nine of us occupied two rooms. The officers had a room on the third floor with a private bathroom. Most of the rooms were alike with a high ceiling and one or more electric fans. Some of the grand suites now had all two or three rooms filled with beds to handle the military overload. The lobby was alive with every kind of human being, and in the room called the Winter Garden, which was the enter of activity, at least part of the population managed to stay drunk from eleven o'clock in the morning until midnight. Liquor was, of course, expensive and not always good.

In that room were English and American civilian workers, European and Eurasian girls from an American Army Services of Supply office. There were occasional sailors, but mostly some pretty rough customers from the Merchant Marine. They weren't a good advertisement with their beards, dirty clothes, loudly foul language, and sloppy inertness after pouring liquor down most of the day, but after a couple of months dodging subs and enemy bombers on a little overloaded boat, I guess they were entitled to do as they damned pleased. There was no doubt that <u>they</u> looked at it that way. There were all the ranks of Allied officers from Colonel down -- the Americans in crisp or wilted khaki shirts, and the British in comfortable "bush jackets", which are very thin cotton blouses. Enlisted men were there, too. The Americans wore row on row of colorful battle ribbons and scattered money all over the table. The British enlisted men were less noticeable. They had been restricted from the hotel until the American enlisted men began coming in with the officers. The English finally had to lower their restrictions and admit their enlisted men.

An orchestra played for two or three hours at meal time, and in an outdoor court called the "Palm Garden", an American negro, Teddy Weatherford, offered some very danceable music.

We had heard of the "300 Club", so we took a taxi there the first night. Like practically all the English clubs where Indian bearers worked, all purchases were paid for with paper coupons bearing the properly stamped amounts. This was a private club which allowed a few officers to come uninvited. There was a small orchestra for dancing, and because of the pleasant atmosphere the "300 Club" was one of the most desirable places to go. The theaters in Calcutta form a large portion of the entertainment. There were about seven, of which three were modernly air-conditioned, plushy, and streamlined, and one was strictly lousy. I use the term with sanguine recollection. Three of the movies I saw during those ten days included "Pardon My Sarong", "The Great Waltz" on return engagement, and "The Fleet's In". American personality suffers in a British theater. They have intermissions like a "legit" or an opera. One is supposed to adjourn to the "bar" and dabble with a lemonade. To me, it was just another twenty minutes worth of callous where it wasn't welcome.

It was not until we walked into the hotel lobby on the second evening and found it in near-panic that we remembered it was Christmas Eve and that we had to obtain special tickets for dinner. Indian clerks were frantically giving out the dinner tickets, trying to restrain the surging of the crowd, fighting for reservations, and keeping the drunks under control.

Shortly after nine o'clock, we headed for our assigned table in the spacious dining room. Almost at the instant we saw that it was already occupied, the air raid sirens blew. The band at one end of the room faltered and two hundred people held their breath waiting for some one to act or give an order. The babble of voices resumed like the rush of Fundy Bay tide, and the orchestra scurried off its platform. The first impulse of all four of us was to go outside and see what was coming off. Since this was the first air raid we had actually been in the center of, we thought that as airmen, some special sanction applied to our movements. I think we finally decided we were too hungry to waste any more time, and took a recently deserted table. Customers and bearers alike had deserted it. The bearers, all but two or three intelligent ones, had run to the kitchen with deathly fear on the black strip of face between white jacket and white turban. Perhaps a third of them were finally admonished -- more likely threatened -- to return to duty. It was one of these wild-eyed, frantically unproductive persons whom we assailed with "Silver l 'ow! Food juldee!"

Barely slowing down, he screamed, "Nay, Sahib, Nay!'

Next we grabbed one of the Anglo-Indian head waiters, and tried to convince him we needed silver and then some soup and then steaks.

"Impossible! Impossible!"

That seemed to be the password. We got it from all the waiters, but we didn't know who to pass it on to.

The lights went out. In a few minutes, the bearers stumbled in with candles, and Ed grabbed one for our table.

I think some of the Tommies there had been in the London blitz by the way they reacted. The customers on the other side of the room were showing signs of being jittery, so two of the Tommies climbed on the band platform and began to abuse a piano and saxophone. About thirty couples jumped up to dance in the dim waver if the candlelight. Everybody around us was still eating, and we wanted to likewise. I grabbed a passing bearer and began to patiently explain what we desired, but Thompson showed him a paper rupee note and spread his hands at the vacancy before him.

There was a gleeful "Yes, Sahib," and in no time at all we had utensils and the first course.

Once I thought I sensed a faint tremor. It was nothing I could feel, but we found ourselves looking at each other momentarily before diving back at the soup. The music seemed to bang a little louder.

Ed waylaid the bearer, and he brought another course of something, but when it came to the steak course, we took Swetland's flashlight and, grabbing another bearer, went to the kitchen. Ed pointed at them, at the bearer, and toward our table.

"L 'ow!" he said. For some reason, the bearer was delightfully on the swing of things. He grinned from black ear to black ear and dumped the whole works out on a serving platter, then followed us to the table.

A little later someone flipped a cigarette into a container of balloons that hung above the dance floor. Hell broke loose for a minute. When we finished the steak course, we gave up and went to bed, wondering if the raid was still on.

My diary entry for December 25the goes like this:

"Merry Christmas! The water's off. The servants are leaving by the thousands. Saw where six light bombs scratched a street, killed two oxen, a few naives and about three British soldiers. Quite a few windows broken. Saw a cinema and went to bed."

The entrances to all buildings on the main streets of Calcutta were blocked by brick bomb walls designed to keep flying fragments out of the stores. White and tan Brahma bulls, turned free through considerations of religion, roamed the main streets at their leisure, spending most of the day in the shade of the brick walls and feeding on the sparse grass on the "Maiden" or central park. No one disturbs the animals, no matter to what extends they block the sidewalks and streets or splatter their excrements about.

Down Chowringee Road goes every kind of vehicle -- 'Rickshaw, taxi, bicycle, horse-drawn gharry, American and British trucks, sometimes tanks, and shiny new American cars belonging to a maharajah or white business man; and Calutta has a streetcar system with more modern equipment than is found in may large American cities. Because of the scarcity of gasoline, most of the cars have a heavy generator fastened on the rear bumper. Into it ground coal is put, and the gas is piped to the carburetor. One of the chief disadvantages is that someone has to tend the thing while the car is parked for short periods so that there will be gas when the driver wants to go,

People starved to death on the streets of Calcutta, and perhaps one or two of the forty Buicks of the young, wealthy, and popular Maharjah of Cooch Biher will have a detour around a body until the proper person can be found to pick it up.

Don't be indignant at the meeting of wealth and a starved body. The cities of the prosperous United States can give you the same scene. But consider the religion that makes it contaminating for the ordinary person to touch the dead. I have seen the bloated bodies of an Indian mother and baby lie in Chowringee Road for three days while traffic routed itself around, and at night lanterns were lit to mark where they lay. The right member of the proper caste had not been found to bury the dead.

The City of Calcutta has a good police force, but some of the techniques used by the Indian police might seem a little rough to us. I have seen a coolie, against whom the evidence seemed incriminating of petty thievery, shake his head frantically, his voice quaver and sob with fear, his eyes grow wild in anticipation of what he knew was coming. But "Nay! Nay! Nay!" was all he could say. He said it with such a terrible, heartrending conviction that I was moved to step in and say, "Look here! Any damn fool can see that man isn't guilty!" But I have seen the police work. They would turn me, perhaps with a condescending smile, saying, "But he is quite guilty, Sir" in the very precise, chi-chi English, which they wear on their tongues with starched discomfort. With a pleasant little nod of his head, the man in charge would permit the beating to start. When it is done with a heavy club on the skin-covered ribs and back of a half-starved man, it sounds like a dull drum. If ribs are broken, as they have been, and no medical attention given, as it seldom is to coolies, the man will probably never be able to do really hard physical labor for the rest of his life. As the beating starts, it is obvious as the passing of film on the movie screen what must be going through the man's mind.

"My chance for wealth is gone for Siva has not delighted in me. I was born with nothing and must die so. Perhaps some day I will be born in wealth. Until then I must live as it is given."

He does not nod to say that he took the money. When he goes limp with resignation, the police tell him to take them to the money, and as often as not he does so. When he goes to his hut, his parents put up a hew and cry, but after a hysterical exchange of Hindustani between them and the police, they quiet down. The hand full of money is given to a fat, flabby faced Indian shopkeeper who has righteously been following the little group. Finally, the accuser has the rightful five dollars back.

Seeing a coolie so beaten, reminded me of a cripple we had seen on the streets of Karachi, who progressed on his elbows and knees. His right leg was emaciated until its diameter was between 1½ and two inches and the foot was uselessly small and bent. There were two startling things about the fellow. One was that his back was apparently broken in the middle where it formed a very sharp angle up to the practically meatless hip bones. The ribs on the left side hung down, while the ribs on the right were parallel with the pavement. The other thing about him was that he always smiled. I think that hurt his capitol stock for begging, because it is hard to toss a coin at a grinning beggar who apparently is enjoying the extent to which his condition plays on your sympathy. There have been times when I wondered whether it was possible that he had purposely brought about his condition. It seems fantastic, so perhaps his god had just been kind to him. Because the caste system puts upon the great multitude of Indians an extreme limitation of pursuit, they turn to begging to live, and it behooves one to be a better beggar than his neighbor. Cases where children have actually been maimed to make them better family beggars are fact.

In Calcutta one day, I saw a sight that made me very sick in the heart. A beautiful Indian girl of 10 or 12 years was leading her tall brother by the hand. The regularity and the softness and the radiance of her features made her a little tan queen in spite of the filthiness of her rags. Her eyes were large and brown and shy as she watched the faces of passers-by to find a glance that would be an opening for her. Ordinarily, people see the beggars ahead of them and are careful to be looking elsewhere when they pass. To look is to be approached and possibly followed down the street. To give is to be besieged by hundreds more.

This little girl, I could not pass. When she saw my glance, she smiled with the faith and anticipation of a little daughter, and quickly reaching one slender arm around her brother's head, with two fingers of each hand, she parted widely the lids covering two sightless hollows. Here was her stock in trade, and feeling very unhappy about what I might be doing to her future, I gave eight annas,

I have heard the Calcutta is named from the Goddess Kali. However, this may be, there is a section of town called Kalighat -- I believe "ghat" means "place by the river", and it was here that we visited the temple of Kali. Until the advent of the British, human sacrifices were a daily occurrence, but now only goats are killed. Kali is called Mother Goddess. It is she who gives life, but evidently she demands life in return.

The temple itself was a small one of marble, standing at one side of a courtyard of stone. The head priest himself welcomed us. He was a tall, thin, cadaverous-looking Indian of light color and sharp noble features. His black hair was dashed with gray, and his muslin clothes were the pale yellow of a priest. As he explained the temple yard to us, I became obsessed with the feeling of eagerness that grew from the man himself. His eyeballs were yellow, streaked with wisps of tan; and his long forefinger, with which he pointed or accentuated a remark, was bony and crooked and longer than any human finger had ever seen. The man spoke perfect English with an Oxford accent -- he had graduated from that school and returned to become a priest of Mother Kali.

A brightly-dressed throng of people milled in wild excitement about the open doors of the temple, but at a clap of the priest's hands, another priest rang a bell, and the throng opened a path so that we could have a glimpse of the goddess herself, but they opened so briefly, that all I was able to see was the colorfulness of her headdress and clothes. Then the crowd closed in again.

The priest kept reminding us that he was now number one temple priest, and he described all the temple's charities to beggars. He showed us the stock in the center of the yard where goats were beheaded and people drank the blood. He neglected to mention that humans had been killed there, too. In one place was a tree from whose limbs small stones hung. He explained that when a woman wanted a child, she brought a small stone, tied it to the tree with a hair of her head, and prayed to Mother Kali. When the child arrived, one of the first things the mother must do was remove the stone, offer a prayer of thanks to Kali, and cut off the child's hair, leaving it at the base of the tree.

In one corner of the yard was an "L" shaped building whose interior was lined with broad stone shelves which were shelters and resting places for women and children. Then, as he accompanied us back to our taxi, he gave the build-up for a big donation to his temple, but it was easy for us to recognize someone else's religion as a racket, and so the donations were small. There had been a note in his talk that indicated that he himself did not believe all he preached

Another interesting spot in Calcutta was the burning ghat where bodies were cremated. It was in a small area between some brick warehouses and the river. As we entered the place, a cremation was getting underway. Beneath a long pyramid of split logs was the cloth-wrapped body of a withered little woman -- her feet were visible at one end and her grey hair could be seen at the other. Three men finished cramming sandalwood shoots under the logs, and then, unconcernedly chanting something, they circled the pyre and ignited the sandalwood from flaming tapers. Professional mourners struck up a clatter with cymbals and drums and chants, and in a recess of a warehouse, the immediate family watched the proceedings. Soon we could hear the sizzle of the body, and smell the burning flesh occasionally above the smell of sandalwood.

From the way everyone watched us, the Americans were more interesting than he wrinkled old woman being sent back to the dust.

You have heard of the lowest caste in India -- the Untouchables. Anyone born into this caste is believed to have committed a sin in a former life, and therefore he is to spend this life in enstonement. He doesn't have a chance from the moment he is born. I don't know what specific jobs they are allowed to do -- perhaps only beggary.

I saw a group of these miserable mortals having their existence on a stretch of sidewalk along one of the broad business streets north of Howrah Bridge. There were between twenty and thirty of them sitting or reclining against a board fence which covered the unsightliness of a vacant lot. The rags they wore were so filthy that I was not sure whether or not the children were the only ones without cover for their black bodies. There was almost no activity along the fence -- the people seemed to be sprawled there waiting for death. That length of sidewalk was their home. Children were born there and old people died there.

I didn't quite know how to compare these people with the coolie or farm class which lived near our camp and whom we knew a little better, but their moral codes were probably similar. The children of these classes are carried about on the hip of the brother or sister who is a little older and able to walk. According to the doctors, this manner of carrying a child tends to increase sexual desire, and the love fests in the spring seemed to bear this out. Near camp large fires would burn all night long, excited voices could be heard, and drums would beat for miles around. The following day, the clothes of the natives would bear splotches of red dye. I gathered from my bearer that the dye was thrown at someone who was about to be chased, whether male of female, and apparently everyone who was unmarried was vulnerable except the small children who could not run fast enough to create interest. It was an open season on love.

I looked again at these people sitting listlessly on the sidewalk and wondered how they could get up energy enough.

It was a relief to leave Calcutta and return to our American camp.

Chapter VIII

SHATTERED GLASS

When Chick Fountain was sent down to India Air Task Force Headquarters in Calcutta, we figured that Ed should be Squadron Commander, but he was out-ranked by two other men on paper and he was young. One of the others became C.O., and the second went into Group Headquarters, while Ed's ability won him one of the best jobs in the Squadron -- that of Operations Officer.

Almost every night there were some good poker games. The stakes seldom were very high, but the games were fun. Major Coleman, the Group Intelligence Officer, was a frequent player. I think he had retired from business in Dayton, Ohio, and volunteered for service. No one enjoyed a good poker game more than he, and he frequently told me what a good player Ed was. Of course, there is a good deal of luck involved and Ed seemed to have plenty of that too.

In February I left the fold of our crew and was given one of my own while Ed got a new co-pilot. My crew was a new one in the Squadrons whose pilots had been a "big operator" or "Hot pilot" in the States. We didn't like the way he flew an airplane, especially the way he lagged in formation. I was made pilot of his crew and he, Bronson, was my co-pilot. He was a very unhappy co-pilot, as might be imagined, since he had been able to pick the finest men of his former squadron for his own crew.

One day when I landed after a mission to Rangoon, Ed met me at the plane with his car, as usual, to take the crew to interrogation. There was something different about him. Ordinarily we sat side-by-side and talked, glancing at each other occasionally. This was a time when Ed was busy, and his face was usually expressionless and intent on what he had to do, but today there was a smug little smile barely hiding beneath the surface. I turned and looked at him closely.

"Well?" he grinned. "What's eatin' on you?"

"Something is certainly gnawing on you, my Friend," I retaliated. "What cooks?"

He tried to sober his face again, but wasn't very successful. Then it suddenly dawned on me. There were two bars on his collar where only one had been for eight months. A captain was a high rank among us.

"Well I'll be damned!" I said, extending a hand. "You got your captaincy! Golly but that's swell!" He could have been no happier than I was. That grin spread like a prairie fire again.

Quite often in the evenings, Swetland and Gimble went into Asensol. At a place called the "European Institute" there were good movies, occasional dances, and a game like "Bingo"

called "Housey". Swetland met a cute Anglo-Indian girl at the dances there and spent occasional evenings with her,

These Anglo-Indians, or Eurasians, are an interesting and in some ways an unfortunate group. They are not really accepted by many of the English or Indians, but they have a much higher place in the society of India than do mulattos in our own society. The Americans in India accepted without question the "Anglos", and it was a common sight to see our men jitterbugging with them at the night spots. Two officers I know intend to marry Anglo-Indian girls when they can be brought to the States.

At a dinner in Burnpur one night, I met a lovely girl whose gayety and charm won all of us. She had black hair and brown eyes and a finely cut nose. Her light tan was becoming -- and it was permanent. She was Anglo-Indian, about three years older than I and her name was Faith Harringan. Her father was an Irishman, her mother an Anglo-Indian, but Faith lived alone in Calcutta, where she was secretary to a tobacco company official. Frequently on weekends she came to Burnpur to visit some friends. I went to a number of dances with her and gradually we became very close friends. I eagerly anticipated my next trip to Calcutta when I could have such an inevitable date.

One night Gimble came home and told me there was a man by the name of Allan Richards who asked if I was in the Squadron. He had received a letter from his mother, who lived next door to my aunt in Chicago, saying there was a William Gilbert in India and wondering if he happened to be near there. The next night I went with Jerry and met this man who became a very good friend of ours. Allan was a heavy-set man of about thirty-four years, who was chief engineer in the rolling mill of the steel plant. As was true of the other Americans and some of the British, his wife had been sent back to the States at the outbreak of war.

We made a good team. He frequently invited us over for home-cooked meals and especially good coffee, which we never had in camp. He lived in a cool apartment where it was pleasant to spend the hot evenings. We brought to him a change of company and no steel talk, and he liked that. Allen had the patience of a mother -- he had to have where his cook was concerned.

"These Indian servants can do some of the damnedest things!" he moaned frequently. "I can show the man precisely what I want done and he will nod his head and say 'Yes, Sa 'ib! Yes Sa 'ib!' and then, damn it, he does exactly as he did before. And he gets nervous when I have guests. Look at those mashed potatoes!" and he banged a spoon against the hard white mass in the dish. "He usually makes fine mashed potatoes. Look at those! He does most of the buying, but he never tells me what he pays. All I know is that he can get things for much less than I can. I'll never forget one time when my wife was here. She was having a special party. She made patty shells for chicken a-la-king and mixed batter for muffins. When the guests arrived Cookee was supposed to start the muffins. A little later she went into the kitchen and I heard the most agonized cry you can imagine: 'Allan, come here!' She didn't know whether to laugh or cry. Cookee had carefully baked the muffins in the patty shells."

The steel mill where Allan worked had been begun by the Germans before the war, It was an Indian-owned company, and the engineers who came with their German blueprints were recalled when war became imminent and they had not finished the construction of the furnaces. The blueprints were burned, and so it was left to American engineers to finish the work and install the rolling mills. The results, as far as the furnaces went, were not an entire success, but they worked.

Allan had some incredible stories to tell. One had to do with stealing by the Indians working in the plant. Zinc became impossible to replace, and it was desperately needed for the steel. An Indian guard was kept on the pile of ingots, but he usually lay down on the pile and went to sleep. One night someone woke the Indian and told him three truckloads of the ingots had been carried away while he slept. Next day the locality was scoured, but the ingots were never found. The remainder of the pile was moved inside the plant and put in a building with a heavy, brass-hinged door to be kept locked. One morning when the men came to work, the door was leaning against the building its brass hinges gone, although the zinc was untouched. Brass of any description -- screws, paper clips, plates, or chair legs -- never lasts long. The Indians made utensils of all sorts out of it. Allan said that a good deal of money is spent buying four-by-four beams eight or ten feet long on which steel sheets are laid out flat to cool. The beams would never wear out, but somehow they slowly disappeared from the plant in spite of the wall and steel fence with guards at every gate and white men who work in the place day and night. There is yet some mystery in the East.

On Wednesday, February 10th, the men of our group formed in front of the control tower on the field to be inspected be General Arnold, who was in India on his tour of the battle zones. Three units of men in their clean, crisp khakis formed in a "U", on one side of which forty-seven of us lined up to receive medals from the General. Although we had already passed our 200th hour of combat, we were to receive the Air Medal for our first 100 hours.

As "Hap" Arnold stepped from his new B-17, we all froze at attention. Our eyes, however, drifted toward the General and the party of men with him. In our group was a Captain by the name of Suggs, who had been an old army sergeant in the Air Corps. This grizzled old man hiked right up to the towering, pink-complexioned, white-haired General, stuck out his hand, and said, with great enthusiasm, "How the hell are ya, Hap!"

We gazed in awed surprise as "Hap", smilingly delightedly, reached out and shook hands with Suggs. We had forgotten that the Air Corps was once a small handful of men who knew each other well, officers and enlisted men alike.

I considered it more of an honor to receive a personal salute and a handshake from that magnificent military gentleman who is head of our Air Force, than to receive the blue and orange ribbon which he pinned on me. Before he left, we gathered in a circle around him to hear his report on plane production and on the other war theatres. He congratulated us on the work we were doing and said he knew we were short of supplies and replacements which was an understated truth, but that a supply line like the tremendous one being pushed into Africa was on its way into India. That was really heartening news, for we had been taking our own planes apart in order to keep others flying. And that word "replacements" was the best morale booster there was. We were sick of India and the war, and "replacements" meant we could go home.

A few months later, Eddie Rickenbacker, sunburned and still so weak from his twenty-one days on a dinghy that he had to be helped from his plane, appeared at the field under similar conditions to pin the Distinguished Flying Cross on us for two hundred hours of combat. Of course the citation was dressed up a little, and for all the men decorated, it read like this.

"...During the period August, 1942 to January 15, 1943, he has participated in combat missions totaling more than two hundred hours. These flights, in which he has flown from bases in India and the Middle East, far over enemy territory, have been eminently successful. By his diligent attention to duty and the superior execution of his assignment as pilot (co-pilot) of a combat team in heavy bombardment aircraft, he has, as a vital part thereof, contributed much to the success of many missions. The operations in which Lieutenant _____ has flown constitute acts of extraordinary achievement in aerial flight and reflect the highest credit to the military forces of the United States."

Rickenbacker's hands still trembled as he pinned on the ribbons, and I could see his knees wobble as he passed down the line of men. He told us the details of his experience adrift at sea and had some pointers to give on ditching a bomber in the ocean. I remember him saying that he deliberately made the men angry to give them additional strength and will to live through the agonies they suffered. The story I heard later from one of the other men in the dinghy verified their anger at Rickenbacker.

There was a tennis court in front of one of our permanent buildings that had been an English residence. All four of us bought rackets and balls, from a Sikh who ran a sports shop in Asansol. There were several other officers who played, and we went at it with terrific vigor in spite of the hot weather. Time after time Ed and I would have close games. If I won several games, I would sometimes make a mistake of betting him ten rupees on the next. That would do it. I almost never won the bet. Sometimes, in my wiser moments, I wondered if I wasn't being set up for a sucker play. I think Gimble was the best player among us, but he felt guilty when he put over his best serve that we could never see coming. When he slowed sown on his serve, the rest of his game slowed down too, and Ed or I could sometimes beat him. Swetland was a careful scientific player who would run the shoes off us if given a chance, but he was not quite fast or hard-hitting enough to offer stiff competition. At first, the court had no fence at either end to stop the balls. The English counted on having the native boys to chase the balls, but we "baksheeshed" them too much and had so many chasing that they would fight over who brought the balls in and would be paid. We had to stop fights to get the balls and continue the game, so we had fences built at both ends of bamboo screens.

I don't remember ever seeing a thermometer in India, except the one in Allan's apartment. I'm sure we would have felt worse to know how hot it really was. The last month in Bengal that was at all cool was January. February was warm. March was hot. In April we were wet with perspiration most of the time and we began to suffer with prickly heat. By May it covered me completely making any clothing uncomfortable until I flew up into cool air. In the middle of the day it was unwise to walk the 500 feet between barracks and mess hall without a sun helmet. The blows of the sun on an uncovered head became like blows of a hammer. Our heavy Khaki kept the sun's rays at bay, but our skin was continually wet and slippery. The first move when returning to the shade of the barracks was to strip to undershorts. Rain had a slight cooling effect, but the oppressive stickiness afterward was miserable. I moved my bed outside in June, during a lull in the monsoon, and frequently lay there with only a mosquito net above and the cotton stripping of the bed below so that I could benefit from any movement of air. The evening breeze sprang up some time after midnight to dry me off and make sleep possible. There was not a fan in camp.

The first heavy rain came late in February and gradually built up into the heavy monsoon of May, June, and July when anything would mold that was not hung in sunlight. During the first part of the monsoon, the rain pounded dully without being augmented by either lightning or thunder. It was spooky to hear only torrents of rain, and in the moist air, the whirling propellers condensed a blue misty circle of droplets that hung just behind the blade tips.

One night as I was walking back to the officers' area from the movie, Sgt. Taylor came up.

"Lt. Gilbert, I got some good new for ya. The enlisted men's club got some ice cream in from Calcutta today. Adam and Chadwick and me are gettin' a gallon and thought maybe you'd like to help us with it." He was practically laughing. We hadn't seen any ice cream in months and he knew darn well the only reason I'd turn down ice cream was if I had to make a choice between that and going home. Adam was already back with the gallon can when we arrived at the half of one of the small brick buildings where all five of our crewmen were quartered.

We had barely pitched into the big can with our little teaspoons, when Chadwick and Filipo and Burns came in. The first two pitched in with us, but Burns was having trouble with diarrhea and preferred just to sit and talk.

"We hardly see you any more since you have your new crew, Lt. Gilbert," Chadwick said. "How are you and Captain Thompson getting along with your tennis?"

"Well," I said, "I always think I'm holding my own until I make a bet with him. Then Bango! There goes ten rupees. Today he beat me ten games to eight. What have you fellas been doing?"

"Well," Filipo answered proudly, "I finally got me an album for my pictures, and I've been pasteing 'em in. Here's the latest picture me girl sent me. Not bad, huh?"

It was the picture of a tall, good-looking Italian girl in a two-piece bathing suit -- the kind of picture that would even boost a man's moral at home. "'Not bad' is an understatement," I said. "Are you engaged to her?'

"Not exactly, Lieutenant, but we kinda got an understanding. I've known her since I was a kid."

Adam had a twinkle in his eye, Like a little boy, he had something on Taylor that was too good to keep. These two still could not refrain from antagonizing each other every so often.

"Boy, did Taylor get poked good last night!"

"G'wan," Taylor retaliated, showing signs of anger. "What d'ya want for two guys against one!"

Adam paid no attention. "For about a week he's been waking up the camp when he comes home drunk from the club and sings louder'n hell. That wasn't no two men last night. That was Baltes. On the way back from the club, he dumped some water in Baltes' bed and then came here and fell asleep. When Baltes come home, he knew who had done it, so he come here and pulled Taylor out of bed. Barker was with him, but he didn't get in the fight. Taylor was standing there swingin' with his eyes still closed. Those dark circles under his eyes aren't from lack of sleep."

"That ain't the way it was either Lieutenant. Adam was sound asleep. I didn't dump water in Baltes' bed. You can ask that redheaded kid next door. I come with him." Taylor got up then, closing that subject, and went to his barracks bag.

"Do you remember when we were in Palestine, Lieutenant Gilbert? I was trying to get a Mauser or Luger gun for you from those Aussies?'

I remembered well, because Taylor had a knack for spending his evenings with Captains, Majors, and Colonels and intriguing them so with his line of chatter that he frequently brought home valuable souvenirs from the front lines as gifts.

He came back with a leather case in his hand and pulled out a handsome German folding desert compass. "Here, Lieutenant Gilbert, I got this just before we left, and I've been meaning to give it to you. I'm sorry I couldn't get a Mauser like you wanted."

I tried to express my appreciation, but he just waved it off. I knew he found deep pleasure in giving and being devoted to the four officers of the crew. He was a gruff little man, but half of him was still boy.

After I had chipped in for my share of the ice cream in spite of their protests, I walked on back to my quarters. Thompson was with Gimble and Swetland in their room next to ours. They had their feet propped up on the tables and were listening to a symphony record Ed had bought in Asansol that day.

"Come on in and pull up a chair, Bill," Gimble offered. "What's the latest rumor about when we go home? Ed says Morse has orders to leave tomorrow. He's over there packing like mad."

"Holy smoke!" I said as I slipped into a chair. "Somebody is finally going home! He has about eighteen months of combat. That leaves only one crew ahead of us. I wonder who blasted higher headquarters loose enough to start shipping men home. Boy! I can hardly believe it! So Morse is finally going home!"

Swetland popped up with an idea. "Say, now that you're not on our crew, I guess you'll have to stay when we go. That's too bad, Bill. You were a nice guy."

I knew he was kidding, but there was a thread of truth in what he said. My face felt starched when I tried to laugh about it. Then, Paul, still teasing, added insult to injury by playing Nelson Eddy's record of "Ride, Cossack, Ride".

About the first of March, I was made Communications Officer. Ordinarily, that job, is held by a ground officer, but we didn't have one who was qualified. The communications section had two functions. One was to maintain contact between the squadron and the group for command purposes. We worked for the group by contacting the other squadrons. The second job was to maintain the radios in the planes and control tower, and to receive messages from a mission returning from Burma. If necessary, we transmitted orders to the planes too.

We had been losing a few planes from another squadron. They seemed to be having pretty bad luck. When planes went down in Burma, they were rarely heard from again. On one occasion, a formation of six ships went into a cloud on their way out of Burma and only five came out. It was that simple. Nine men and a bomber gone and we were never sure what happened.

On another occasion, we were on our way into Rangoon by the water route while the other squadron was leaving directly across the land. They were using the same frequency for inter-plane communication that we were, so we heard them talking and knew that after leaving the targets they were jumped by three Zeros. The motor of one ship had been damaged by ack-ack and finally had to be feathered so that the plane dropped behind in formation before the other ships knew about it. The Zeros closed in for the kill and over the air came the frantic calls of the doomed pilot asking the formation to slow up so that he could stay with them.

The call became a scream as he recognized the presence of death: "Wait! Wait! They've got my waist gunners! Slow up! I've got three Zero's on me!" It was too late. In a minute he no longer transmitted.

A pilot in one of our other squadrons had a navigator who considered himself an atheist. He gambled excessively, winning and losing sums of money that sometimes ran as high as $1000 a night many nights in a row. Sometimes in the heat of aerial combat over Burma, when four or five pursuits were attacking from different directions and the pilot was struggling over controls and throttles, the navigator would pause in the acrid smoke of his nose gun to call up the pilot on the interphone and shout: "See that plane at two o'clock high coming in? Well, if there's a God, have Him strike that plane down!" Then grimly he would bend over his gun again. This occasional fanatical outburst from the nose of the ship brought an added strain of anger to the busy pilot, but he made no effort to get a new navigator because by the time the flight was over he was cooled off sufficiently to allow the other man his own troubled concept of the way of things.

"The way of things" sometimes had a particular cruel manner of operating. Swetland received a letter from a navigator in our old squadron near Benghazi, saying Lewis, a pilot we all knew, had been shot down near Malta. At almost the same hour, his son had been born at home in New Mexico.

In our own squadron we had been kidding a boy named Garrett about his approaching fatherhood -- how he would have to bounce the kid on his knee by V-mail. While Garrett was on a mission, the telegram finally arrived. That night the Squadron Commander read it: "Congratulations! You are the father of an eight pound boy!" Garrett didn't return.

These were men we didn't live with. We had seen them, talked to them, and knew them by name. Our squadron had been lucky. I guess we thought that was a sign of our planning missions better or flying them better.

On March 12th an order came in for us to send everything we had against a bridge near Rangoon on the next day. I remember the thoughtful expression of Ed's face when the Engineering Officer told him only four planes were ready to fly and it was too late in the evening to have more ready by daylight. Ed didn't want to send four planes over Rangoon, but orders are not to be questioned. He took the lead plane himself. Henry Root volunteered to take the last one, and when Anderson and Welfare, the other two pilots, were told there would be only four of them, their jaws quietly clenched and they nodded, because it was their turn to go. Late that night, Ed said, "Damn it! I feel I shouldn't go tomorrow, then joined the poker game for an hour and won fifteen dollars. Before I went to bed I gave him the communications flimsies I had prepared, giving radio frequencies and recognition signals for four planes, number twenty-one, twenty-two, twenty-three, and twenty-six.

It was dark when the alarm by Ed's bed went off. I awoke long enough to hear the scrape of his heavy shoes as he put them on, and their scuff as he went out to wake the other officers and go to breakfast. I can hear yet the click of his gun belt as he fastened it on, and the dingle-dangle made by his dog tags, I think I mumbled, "Good luck." I hope I did. Saying nothing, he went out to the truck with his jacket over his arm. I remember seeing his silhouette against the truck's headlights. In the dim anticipation of dawn, I awakened briefly as the flight droned overhead. Four sets of synchronized engines make a beautiful sound. I went back to sleep for a few hours.

In the afternoon, I was down at the radio shack when the messages came in from two planes, numbers twenty-one and twenty-three. Those were Anderson and Welfare. Twenty-two and twenty-six never reported.

Anderson's message said he had one man dead and another seriously wounded. He stopped at Calcutta to get his gunner to a doctor and a hospital quickly. Welfare was low on gas and was landing near the coast. Later that night we knew that Ed and Henry had been shot down. The details came the next day with the arrival of Anderson and Welfare themselves and their nervously exhausted crews.

The formation had been jumped by two Zeros while they were on the bomb run. The pursuit planes were not expected so soon, and they came straight down from the sun. One of Ed's motors was knocked out and was immediately feathered. Another must have been damaged because the plane made a violent lurch to one side, loosening up the formation. The top turret, that would be Chadwick, was firing until after the second attack. Then it ceased.

Henry had one motor on fire and another feathered as the planes turned and dived toward the Gulf. In the confusion of the moment, Anderson and Welfare were not sure on whose wing each reassembled. The lead plane could not hold altitude -- one moment it would almost stall and then it would dive. They were under hard-pressed attack for about twenty minutes, and shortly before the two planes hit the water, the pursuit turned back and was lost in the haze. Both pursuits were damaged.

The B-24's made controlled landings on the water a few miles apart, but the force of impact broke them up. Some of the gas tanks and wing sections floated but no dinghies were seen to appear. Three men were spotted at the wreckage of one plane, but one was riding high in the water with his yellow Mae West. Five men appeared from the other plane. Anderson and Welfare circled and dropped their own life jackets, but the dinghies would only release to the outside where they would catch the two vertical stabilizers and endanger the whole plane, probably taking off the tail section. For the sake of the men still flying, the rafts could not be released.

The two planes finally had to turn and leave, knowing there was no chance for the men in the water. They were in heavy haze, twenty-five miles form the Burmese shore and without a dinghy. We had no craft that could reach them, and the Japs probably did not know they were there.

When I knew the story, an incoherent tangle of emotions began to writhe inside me. Physically, I felt weak in my legs and in my stomach, and my thoughts held their knowledge with cold fingers. It was like seeing an object that is occasionally obscured by patches of fog, so that you are not sure what is dream and what is true. It actually was several days before it did not seem foolish to say that Tommy and Bill and Jerry and Henry and the rest were gone. It was a hushed camp because every man was having a struggle with himself. I don't think

Anderson was physically capable of flying a mission for a month after the second man of his crew died in the Calcutta hospital.

My own head was too muddled to know whether it had a logical sequence of thoughts. I was scared and awed at the presence of Death in our living quarters where little personal things like scribbling on a pad and a knot I saw tied in a shoelace took on a vicious silence.

We kept saying, "If they come back," and we knew they would not, but that made a temporary little step in the big transition. It was nearly a week before I made myself put their things away and write the letters home giving a fuller explanation than the cold War Department words "Missing in action."

I tried to overlook the fact that I had been lucky -- and I felt guilty that I had left my crew.

So, in the long run Ed's luck had let him down. Is all life like a poker or crap game based on probability? Do millions of influences make us jump around like popcorn on a hot stove, or is this a willful world? If so, the God whose Son would suffer little children to come unto Him has a cruel will.

Then suddenly I realized that in myself there bloomed a substantial clump of those smiling lovely flowers of sheltered existence that had made millions of Americans think "It can't happen to me! Those things happen in stories and to other people, but not to me." I was amazed at the fragile window of glass I had been hiding behind. I could comprehend the war and what we had fought for -- it was all very reasonable. People were bound to be killed. I had even been afraid for my own life more than a few times, but when I came home alive from each mission, a jovial face popped up on my side of that glass shield and said, "Well, what did you expect? <u>You</u> didn't really think <u>you</u> would die?" Then I felt ashamed that I had weakened, and turned again to my protected view of ack-ack bursts and enemy pursuits beyond my glass armor.

But Ed and Jerry and Paul and Adam and Taylor and all the rest of the crew were on my side of that glass window. The crash of that fragile transparent armor still reverberated in my ears, and now that view of enemies and guns and falling and death were there with nothing between. I would die now, too. Alternately, I didn't give a damn, and then I was scared to numbness. To die means giving up identity -- giving up the smiling warmth of that sun, and the smell of earth after rain, and finding the girl I would marry someday. The world is too interesting to leave just because the lines of probability and enemy gunfire would cross in the Universe where I was to be sitting.

Our bad luck had only started. The next was Bronson's, whose crew had been given back to him. He straggled in formation and was shot down by two fighters. Because his ship caught fire, the men had to bail out, but in spite of the fact that the enemy planes circled the men as they dropped, they apparently did not fire at the dangling men, although they heavily machine-gunned the plane when it crashed.

The monsoon began to keep us out of the sky regularly, but sometimes we could fly below the clouds at 500 feet and dodge the rain showers. In this manner we could patrol the shipping lanes, but not go into Burma itself. The two times that we did find ships, we were able to climb in a hole in the clouds and bomb from 7000 feet, but visibility was always bad.

300 hours of combat was the goal we strived for. It might be possible for us to go home then, but nothing had definitely been stated.

I was superstitiously scared about the mission that would give me over 300 hours. It seemed ominous even to think that it might be my last mission. Although we were jumped by two I-45s that kept drilling closer and closer with their noses aflame with firing cannon and giving off a thin streamer of smoke that trailed from their guns, the worst battle was the weather on the way home.

We had been able to bomb Rangoon, but had to descend to 1000 feet to fly home beneath the terrific weather. It was too rough to use the autopilot, and the co-pilot and I took turns for four hours. The rain pounding on the metal and plexi-glass drowned out the vibration of the four motors. The vibration came from blasts of rain. We could see nothing ahead but below the sea was gnashing lone white teeth. The motors seemed to churn through gray water, not through air. The long slender wings flapped in the violent air currents until the tips displaced an arc totaling more than six feet. With each terrific jerk, I was sure the main spar would break, and it was a short 1000 feet to the water below. Everybody was frightened, and they had a right to be. It was more of a beating than a plane was built to stand, and a B-24 was built to stand plenty. The year before, the short stubby wind of a B-17 had been buckled in a monsoon, so I didn't think this long slender one stood a chance. Thinking it might be less violent down at 500 feet, I tried going down there but we hit an air pocket and dropped a good portion of the distance to the water. That was enough. I climbed back up quickly. At one time the rain was so hard the wing lost its lift, and even with additional power, I could barely hold altitude.

The skill and muscle that we put into our survival were negligible factors in the outcome. The judge of the winner between the plane and the elements was Time. Time -- time -- time must pass. How long could the wings flap so violently and stay on the plane? How long could the motors turn? How soon would we fly out of the weather?

Intense ack-ack lasts for only a few minutes -- pursuit for little more than an hour at most. But weather is as violent and deadly as the enemy at his worst, and it lasted four hours. I was glossy and slippery with sweat. It ran in a ticklish stream down my back and dripped from my bare arms onto the radio switch box. My arms and shoulders and back, ached as they had never done, even though I flew only thirty minutes at a time. My thin, wiry co-pilot was no better off.

Time gave the decision to the wings and the motors and the insignificant men. The rain stopped, the black clouds grew light, and we suddenly broke out into bright blue daylight near the coast below Calcutta

Everyone on board became wreathed with the newfound smile of the skies, and we were in a state of nervous hilarity when the tires screeched onto the cement landing strip. I pushed back the window for fresh air, and was greeted by the sound of the calmly idling motors. With throaty confidence they said they were ready to start again. But I weakly shook my head. I wasn't.

Chapter IX

TWO OF THE EAST

It was a week after Thompson and Root went down that I met Phil Roberts. He was the kind of trouble-shooter you find in the technical fields who is like a new V-8 engine under the battered hood of a rusty model T Ford. The fellows would ask who the sad sack was, and I explained he was there at General Haynes' direction to establish a communication system as efficient as Chennault's in China. I imagined he was about thirty with a thin angular nose and a face to match. On the filthiest officer's flight cap I have ever seen was the bar of an American warrant officer. He needed a shave, his shoulder sagged, his shirt drooped, and his hands and pants were greasy, a shiny black gun belt and loaded holster sagged around his thin hips almost to the position of a girdle. The belt was lined with bullets, and the holster held a beautiful .38 automatic. Before we checked over my communications section, I persuaded him he would be more comfortable if I locked his gun and belt in my footlocker.

The more I talked to Roberts, the better I like him. He was honest and unassuming, but quite definite on how the communications system should be handled. He liked his liquor, and after work we spent a good deal of time at the bar in our officers' mess. We had no whiskey, but the brandy and gin and liqueurs were good.

After dinner and before it grew dark, we took our guns and drove in my jeep to a small wooded area where jackals were known to be. The animals would sit at the edge of the area waiting for it to grow dark enough to cover their trips across open country in search of food. By the time we saw them, they were slinking back into the wood, and we only managed to wound two of them.

When it turned dark, Roberts and I drove into Asansol and spent the evening at Madath's, drinking American champagne by the bottle. It was the only palatable drink in the place. Madath was a slippery Armenian who had been about to retire before the war, but suddenly found his grocery and restaurant business to be a gold mine. He could not make himself retire from such easy money as scarce items brought from American soldiers who had a limited chance to spend their money.

Roberts had a Chinese wife who was in Japanese-occupied territory, and he was worried about getting her out. Through the missionaries, he occasionally received notes from her, but he had not seen her since January of 1942, when he left to join the British Army in Rangoon. He was in time to start the long walk out of Burma.

On about the first of April, Roberts, who was a second lieutenant in the British Army, was in Myitkyna, north of Mandalay. He was waiting to be ferried across the river when word came to Signals that the Japs were coming. There was no time to wait for the slow overcrowded ferry. The car he was in belonged to a friend in the A.V.G. (1st American Volunteer Groups known as the "Flying Tigers" were volunteer air units, organized by the United States government combined forces with China in the bombing of Japanese cities, commanded by Claire Lee Chennault) who had two Burmese wives and two children. The wives didn't want to leave Burma, so the American decided to put them in a village and to hide himself nearby. The last Roberts saw of them, they were sitting by the road eating breakfast out of tins. He took the car and drove 30 miles to the east where the road ended. There he found several other cars and a great many Chinese men and two women, all of whom were intending to spend the night in a house there and leave by foot for China the next day. The Chinese couldn't see why Roberts wanted to go to China, but after much talking, they finally accepted him.

Everyone slept the night on the floors of the house, and in the morning the pack train they were expecting arrived from China. Roberts threw away all his clothes except what he wore and a change of underwear. Using his British army blanket and two others, he made a pack, tied with a rope. He had an Enfield rifle, a musette bag filled with ammunition, papers, and a towel. On one hip was a .45 automatic and on the other was the .38. Just before leaving, he poured gasoline on the car and burned it.

The advance party consisted of Roberts; the Chinese leaders Shan and Nelson Tan; Miss Young, a Chinese nurse, and her shy boyfriend; a Chinese man and his pregnant wife; and six mules. They started off single file up a mule train out in the rock that wound up the first mountain of the trip. In the afternoon, they began to grow terrifically tired from lack of food, because they had not stopped for lunch. They passed over the ridge of the mountain and descended into a cool jungle, and, just as the advance group reached the Burmese town they had intended to stay at, they heard machine gunning. And later they discovered that a Jap plane had strafed the rear of their column, killing two Chinese. Three miles past the town, they built a fire to cook rice, and then bought cramped sleeping room in a Burmese house. They had accomplished eighteen miles that first day.

The second day the party traveled twenty miles through thick jungle and across many streams. They had had a quick breakfast of rice, but carried some cooked rice to eat as they walked. At the town where they spent the night, there was a British Indian camp across a gorge, but they didn't want to cross the gorge to stay there, and at that time there was some doubt in Shan's mind as to which trail they should take in the morning, although the matter was cleared up before the time to leave. On the third day Robert's party traveled across open country and started up the 6000-foot slope of a mountain range. They reached the cold top at four in the afternoon, and Shan said that China lay below. Part way down the eastern slope was the custom inspector's house where they spent the night. Everyone was cold, so the inspector, a genial fellow, prepared hot coffee and gave them some brandy.

On the fourth day they traveled twenty-four miles, but were too tired by nightfall to walk the last ten miles into Tengchung. Most of the distance had been across rice paddies and through jungles. The pregnant woman had the equipment thrown off one of the mules so she could ride, but she fell off and was then carried by some paid Burmese natives who seemed as wild as animals.

As they were starting for Tengchung the next morning, they heard that the Japs were about to take the town, but since the Chinese they met continually spread alarms about the Japs, Roberts went toward the town to find out for himself. As he approached the town, he heard rifle shots and a great many people with packs were coming down the road toward him. Roberts could not persuade anyone to stop and tell him what the trouble was, so he finally threatened them with his rifle, and had to slap them to get answers to his questions. He determined at last that the Japs were in the town with their machine guns set up, so he returned to the party and held a council of war. Shan suggested burning all their papers and passports and going into town. In order to dissuade him from this move, Roberts told horror tales about what the Japs had done to Chinese who had worked for white men. He wanted to go north around Jap-held territory, but the Chinese were afraid of "wild men" up there. After seeing the Burmese who were carrying the woman, he had an idea of what they meant, but thought it was the only chance.

The mule driver wanted to go into town with the obvious intention of selling his goods as well as the party to the Japs. He grew stubborn and would do nothing else until Roberts fired a bullet near his head. That changed his mind. The party then proceeded north to the Marco Polo trail, said to be the trade route established by Marco Polo and was much wider than any other. It took them three days to go fifty miles north to the trail and the natives they met there were hostile and had to be threatened for food. All of them had terrible goiters. They would take no less than one hundred Chinese dollars for a chicken. At the time that was about one dollar American.

Chinese soldiers continually passed them and spread stories about what the Japs had done at Tengchung, and that they were coming north up this trail. Roberts said this three-day stretch was the roughest they had yet been over. They were all wet and cold when they reached the Marco Polo trail, so they rented a house and slept on the board floors upstairs to avoid rats.

At midnight, a Chinese soldier woke them, saying the Japs were only eight miles down the trail. In fifteen minutes the party was moving. A few hours later they reached the broad Marco Polo trail which showed its centuries of use, particularly where the trail went up or down by means of stone steps and the rock was worn six inches deep in the shape of a human foot. Still they passed through jungles that were like a green tent, and mountain ranges, and across broad plains. Climbing the mountains was like spending a slow dismal lifetime at hard labor, and on down the slopes it became difficult to keep from running and blistering the feet.

Robert's heels were blistered badly, so he cut off the heels of the shoes. Twice when they were going down the mountain slopes by the deeply worn steps, donkeys slipped against the jagged rocks along the path and ripped themselves open.

The nurse had thrown her shoes away and was walking barefoot. She limped a slight bit, but had no pack to carry as the others did. Whenever they came to a stream, she had to stop and dip her feet a while to cool them off, and at times she grew disgusted with the terrific effort of their march and refused to go farther. Once when she was sitting like this on a rock, a large, gaunt gray wolf appeared and began to creep toward her from behind. When her companion saw the wolf, he was too frightened to move or shout, but just by chance Roberts looked toward her, saw the danger she was in, and quickly killed the wolf with his Enfield rifle. The sudden shot made her jump, but even when she examined the large furry body, she showed no fear. The Chinese boy still trembled and would not go near the animal.

That night they camped on the trail because the Chinese seemed particularly afraid of the jungle. They were growing short of food because one of their donkeys had fallen over a cliff with his load of rice.

It took a day and a half to reach the top of the next mountain and people were very tired, but because the natives said the Salween River was only six miles ahead, they pushed on until eight that night. At eight o'clock the party gave up and all crowded together on Robert's blankets to sleep.

The next day they could see the river eighteen miles away. It was hard to remain at a walk on the down slope, and the manner of walking made the knee bones sore. Roberts went ahead to the river and slept until the others arrived. The riverbanks bore extremely wild jungle. The river was about 150 yards wide and very swift, but a ferry operated there, and they made arrangements to go across at five that night. The boat left the bank at a point upstream, and drifted quite a way downstream before it could be paddled to the other side. Then it was towed upstream again for the next trip.

On the far side, they met an engineering party of five men who thought Roberts should go with them and try to hit the

Burma Road at a point east of Paoshan. After talking with Shan, he decided to go with the engineers.

So the following day they followed the Salween River toward Paoshan. The way was through jungle, but toward late afternoon, they reached a Chinese temple on a high ridge, and because it was raining like the devil, they went inside to spend the night.

It rained all the next day, and by five o'clock they reached a Chinese Army camp where the men were sleeping under trees, in sheds, and in pigpens. In the next several days, the party crossed many streams, rice paddies, and went through many deserted villages. They came to a famous town of temples (I believe it was Tali) where there was a wonderful road of packed clay twelve miles long and a hundred feet wide. A local Chinese governor had built it 200 years before, and Roberts made the mental note that it would be perfect for a runway.

There were two more days of traveling over mountains before they reached a village thirty miles north of the Burma Road and fifty miles east of Paoshan. At that time they didn't know whether the Japs had Paoshan, but they knew they did have Chungling, which was to the north.

The other men of the party were tired and afraid to go on to the Burma Road, but Roberts decided it would be all right. The local magistrate, who was also town mayor and number one schoolteacher, decided that since Roberts was headed for Kunming and the A.V.G., he should be given a party. Out came the village's supplies for rice, pork, and tea, and it was really a party.

That night he slept on a hard board bed. In the morning, he didn't want to wash and shave off his growth of whiskers -- he was growing quite fond of them. They put him on a little donkey, and with his feet trailing the ground and a Chinese soldier leading him, he started on the two-day trip to the Road.

It rained continually, and he shivered until he thought he would fall apart. Every so often, when he came across a hut, he would dismount and go in. The people would be sitting in front of smoldering sticks, and when he tossed on an armful of wood to make a fire that would dry him out, the people just watched and said nothing.

Finally he reached the town of Weyo, which was the stopping place of the trucks on the Burma Road. Here a Chinese Major questioned him until he was satisfied that Roberts was going to the A.V.G., and then he put him in someone else's place on a loaded truck bound for Shangwan, where there was a hostel belonging to the American Technical Group that was engineering the Burma Road. There he ran into a Chinese Colonel from Nashville, Tenn., by the name of Peter She. They had known each other in Loywing, but Roberts was so ragged and dirty that the Colonel recognized him only by his voice. A Dr. May of the 4th ambulance Unit, who had just escaped from Burma, cleaned and doctored his blistered feet. Then a Chinese nurse put him to bed and fed him coffee and cheese sandwiches. He stayed there for three days until some of his strength returned, then was taken in an ambulance to the outpost of the A.V.G., and from there was flown to Chennault in Kunming.

In five minutes after seeing Chennault, he had a job -- straightening telephone lines near the Kunming headquarters. He started that afternoon, but didn't get very far. He was dizzy and uncomfortable in his body because of the sudden acquisition of good food after weeks on a rice diet.

The last time I saw Phil was in Calcutta. He had received word that his Chinese wife was en-route to Kunming, and Phil was straining at the leash to end his assignment in India,

Not long after Roberts left, I became Mess and Bar Officer for the Squadron, and made frequent trips to Calcutta by truck. The hotels were usually crowded. It was difficult to place reservations with them, and it was almost impossible to obtain a bed immediately upon arrival.

The relation between Faith and myself had steadily grown beyond academic friendship -- we didn't intent to be platonic; and when she found I would be appearing in Calcutta frequently, she suggested I stay with her. I had expected her to ask, and if I once had compunctions against accepting such an offer, the environment of India and my long absence from female companionship had softened my resolutions. I asked her if she wasn't endangering the esteem of her neighbors.

"Why, William Gilbert," she chided me, over-emphasizing the "l" in my last name as Anglo-Indians do. "You sound absolutely prissy! That is not frowned on here, but I don't want you to feel uncomfortable about it."

I blurted an approval before the offer could be withdrawn. After all, I was a big boy now.

I usually arrived in Calcutta by mid-morning, established my driver in a building assigned to American enlisted men stationed there, and told him where to meet me at 1:00 the following day. Then I called Faith at her office, and spent the afternoon accumulating supplies.

I pounded my feet to blisters on the near-molten pavement of Calcutta streets, ricocheting from supply house to supply house, driven by the charge of terrific prices. Whatever prices were, I could pay for what the officers really wanted, because the money came from their pockets. But there were two considerations that made constant comparison and haggling worthwhile, although my monetary gains were small. In the first place, even supplies that were present in large amounts in Calcutta were sold in small quantities by the Indian merchants. When I returned for a duplicate order, the price had risen. Buying from someone else who had not yet raised his price could save money, but he was a difficult man to find. If we made no effort to hold prices down, we would soon be unable to buy at all. The second reason was that the very presence of the Americans and their careless spending was imposing unfair difficulties on the British who received a fixed income, and it was cause for much bitterness against us. In general the American attitude was "What the hell do I care" and the British knew it.

Faith arrived home from work shortly after five o'clock. "Home" was a single room of fair size in one of the large apartment buildings just off Chowringhee Road. This room was bedroom and living room, a two-burner stove in one corner was the kitchen, and the bathroom washbowl was ample and served a dual role as kitchen sink.

By six thirty or seven, we were cleaned up for the evening, and the first stop was the porch off the main dining room at "Firpo's" -- one of a chain of choice Eastern restaurants and pastry stores. Here was the only place where gin became a real

Tom Collins with sugar and fresh lemon instead of "lemon squash", a universally used artificial flavor.

While Faith and I sat here, watching the passers-by or the Chinese boy-acrobats on Chowring Road below, or the assortment of nationalities and uniforms at the tables about us, we talked of ourselves, our backgrounds and how our countries were different.

Faith was born in the northern town of Simla, but after going to public schools, she spent most of her time working in Rangoon as a typist and there was engaged to an English boy. She told of the weekend trips and picnics they and their friends enjoyed, and a sparkle always lighted her brown eyes as she spoke. Sometimes the sparkle went out of focus, and I knew her eyes were wet. But Faith was too strong and dynamic to really cry. Those happy days in Rangoon had ended first with his death from some rapidly consuming disease, and finally by the Japanese occupation of Burma.

Faith was a great many fine things. She was brilliant at her job as a secretary, and had risen nearly as far as a businesswoman can in India. What she really wanted was marriage and a family, but there were few men capable of being her husband and fewer who would prejudice their futures by marrying an Anglo-Indian. She did not really expect to find such a man, and had turned down several offers of marriage.

Faith had a right to bitterness, but the flame of it licked out mainly at the petty men at her office who tried to push their entire work onto her already full day. If they had no raise in salary or position to offer, she spiritedly said, "You can just go along with your work!"

When our conversations ran down, she would dust off and recolor the petty problems of the day, saying "The cheek of that man, Bill, trying to get me to take on his silly work! Lord knows I have plenty of my own to do."

Sometimes we ate at Firpo's and danced there, or just as often dined at the Grand Hotel and danced to Teddy Wetherford's music in the Palm Garden. Faith became a little schoolgirl when she danced -- she loved to dance the American way with bodies close, and in moving perfection to American rhythm. The English dance a bit differently than we do, but the thing that is hard for us to become used to is dancing two feet apart.

An English girl once said, "I hope you won't think me bold, but why do Americans always dance so close?" I told her it was easier for a boy to lead and a girl to follow that way, and you could talk into each other's ear instead of shouting for the whole room to hear. Since Americans have danced around the world, I imagine many English girls have accepted our way.

Sometimes Faith and I took a horse-drawn gharry and went clip-clopping through the Lilliputian streets of China town to the Peking Restaurant and the best Chinese food I have ever eaten. There were always good movies to see too.

Then it was time to go home, and we would squeeze into the seat of a rickshaw as she gave the boy directions in Hindustani. She told me the life expectancy of these rickshaw wallas was ten years for they soon develop tubercular cough.

Faith was an important person among her friends. A nearby couple was in the throes of severing their marriage but it was Faith who could talk to them and chide them and bind them together again. And there was a mother whose boy had lain unconscious in the hospital for three months with malaria and a heart complication. The boy looked like death itself, and the mother was ready to give up. But Faith would not let her give up. It was she who gave her renewed courage to stay by her boy -- and he pulled through, although when I saw him he still looked like a living skeleton that managed to maneuver on two feet.

Faith was a remarkable part of India which I shall never regret having known, though she had the Western attitude of intermingled compassion and aloofness for the deep problems burdening the low castes of India -- and thereby all of India.

Chapter X

REST CAMP

In the hill regions that border northern India and in Kashmir, there are numerous towns to which in peacetime the British population moves for the hot summer months. During the war, chiefly army wives populated the places and a few troops, leaving room for American rest camps. The one I went to was called "Ranikhet," northeast of Delhi, fourteen miles from the Tibet border. When notice arrived that two officers from our Squadron would accompany the enlisted men there, a Lt. Shores and myself were selected. We were taken into Asansol to board a special train with the British troops from the area.

In accordance with the segregation of ranks that is practiced in the English Army, and is supposed to be practiced in our Air Forces, the officers were given two or three cars with first and second compartments, while the enlisted men drew something less comfortable. A third class car in India is nothing more than a freight car with many windows and the interior floor space crowded with wooden benches, The G.I.s had to travel and eat and sleep in those cattle cars for two and a half days.

On the station platform were supplies we divided up between the cars. There was bread, cans of beans, peaches, sardines, pineapple, stew, crackers, and many more things. We could not depend on getting any food at the stations where the train stopped to refuel, although at the larger towns many bearers would rush up to the train windows to take orders for tea, fish, or eggs, and in a few minutes they would hurry back with a tray-full for us. It was like curb service.

At Barielly, we changed to a narrow gauge railroad of excellent quality, and in a few hours we unloaded at the town of Kathgodam.

Have you ever ridden in a truck along a narrow mountain road where you can look up the steep incline of a mountain on one side and down a steeper cliff on the other? And the road was full of hairpin turns in recessed perpendicular gorges? And been driven by someone who has just learned how and is not sure of himself? We started out in a convoy of about thirty trucks driven by Indian soldiers who had spent many -- but not enough -- weeks shortly before learning to drive. When we reached the camp hours later, half the trucks had American G.I.s at the wheel with slightly embarrassed and sometimes indignant Indians sitting next to them. The place where I wanted to take over, but didn't, was a sharp turn in a gorge where the driver pointed down and said a truck of this convoy had gone over the day before. "Gone over" meant banging down a steep incline of bare rock for 1000 feet before dropping through sheer space for 2000 more. I don't know what it hit then -- it didn't make any difference.

The town of Ranikhet looked as though it had been plastered on the side of a mountain and there it stuck. Above it, where the mountain leveled out slightly, was the English settlement -- a beautiful spot with hills, winding roads, and woods.

The American camp was for the G.I.s -- there were horses they could rent from the Indians, and places to play tennis and golf. One of the main attractions was the Red Cross Canteen run by "Pop" Tracy. It was a big success. In a land where there is not real hamburger meat nor the right buns to put hamburgers on, "Pop" had produced both, and the biggest hamburgers I have ever seen, with all the "fixin's", sold for about six cents. "Pop" also arranged weekly dances, and by pure high-pressure salesmanship persuaded the married and unmarried women of the settlement to come stag to the dances. "Pop's" canteen was a real success. We were glad to see the Red Cross achieve something, for we had only unfortunate experiences with some of their representatives to judge that organization by.

There were only five officers in camp, and we joined the pleasant English club so that we could play tennis and golf, see plays, attend the dances, and enjoy bar facilities. Liquor was rationed, and we received an equal ration with the regular members. Out the back door of this Ranikhet Club, the beautiful snow-capped peaks of Tibet, which towered above the nearer mountains, formed a jagged horizon eighty miles away.

The main event of my stay there was a hunting trip arranged by the Special Services Officer. Four of us -- Van Pelt and Gabriel, who were sergeants in charge of my Communication Section, and a Sergeant Hank Mueller who was Mess Sergeant at our base, and myself -- were taken sixteen miles along the mountain from Ranikhet to a little village called "Betronj Khan," saddled on a ridge between two mountain ranges. Here we were left with our guide, Rajah Singh, and five days' equipment including food, blankets, Garand rifles, and ammunition.

While Rajah Singh searched for someone with packhorses, we wandered about four hundred feet in town, exchanging stares with the inhabitants. There was one beautiful little girl who seemed very friendly, and Gabriel wanted to take her picture, but the minutes she saw the camera she ran to the protection of her parents who stood laughing in front of their house. Gabe had offered her an anna to let him take her picture but when she refused he gave it to her anyways. Her parents felt that since she accepted the coin she should pose for the picture, and they urged her forward until she finally broke out crying.

When Rajah Singh returned, we loaded all our equipment on the horses and descended 3500 feet down a trail on which a jeep would just fit. After six miles of skidding descent on the gravel footing, we arrived at the inspector's cabin where we were to stay. It was near a small village, called "Baitalghat", on the Kosi River, a swift but broad and shallow mountain stream. The cottage was a handsome little stone building with two sleeping rooms, and open porch, and little else.

The horse had barely sagged to a standstill to wait unloading, when the yard of our cabin was crowded with the assistants of Rajah Singh. For the most part they were coolies to bring wood and water and to act as bearers for our hunts. One of these Rajah Singh sent off to buy two goats to be used as bait. He was determined to start our hunt for leopards that night, and though my feet were blistered from the downhill walk, I agreed to go with him.

I like goats. I had known little about them before I came to petting terms with the one we were to use that night. He was nearly all black, and no matter what befell him he remained unemotional and supercilious. He watched us calmly from under the base of his short horns, although the constant quirk at the corners of his mouth seemed to indicate exasperation. When I would caress his long silken ears, he would nuzzle his wedge shaped head into my stomach, close his eyes blissfully, and go off to sleep so soundly that his legs fell out from under him and he woke just as his knees touched the ground.

Before dark, Rajah Singh and I, and a coolie boy leading the goat, walked about two miles down the river to a place where a small plateau two hundred feet high sat like a footstool between a tall mountain and the river.

Selecting an open place with a large bramble bush nearby, Rajah Singh cut a small entrance into the bush, enlarging the interior to make room for the two of us, while the boy tethered the goat in the open area, being careful to have the goat facing the other way when Rajah Singh and I crawled into our blind. The boy camouflaged the front of the blind with cut bramble and then departed.

At first the goat seemed loath to believe that he had actually been tied in this wild place and left alone. Although the expression on his face never altered, he tugged at the rope and looked alertly in all directions searching for one of us. We in the blind only fifty feet away were choking in an attempt to stifle our laughter at the goat's concern. It was like playing hide-and-go-seek when the one who is "it" is practically stepping on you without knowing it.

At first the goat rasped out a few bahs, but as darkness came on, he realized silence was golden and lay down quietly. Soon we could scarcely make out the contour of the goat against the black landscape even when we lowered our line of vision to put the slightly less black sky behind him. Our quarters were cramped, and we had to be careful how we straightened a leg in order to maintain silence. I could hear frogs and crickets from miles away, but nothing else. The weight of my rifle on my knee put my lower leg to sleep, and I frantically tried to rub the prickly sensation away soundlessly.

Once we heard the hollow roar of a cat from way up the mountain, and Rajah Singh touched my arm significantly. I nodded. Hours passed. The goat was motionless -- probably asleep. Mosquitoes buzzed around us and the frogs and crickets were screaming at each other for miles up and down the river.

Suddenly Rajah Singh leaned forward and grasped the flashlight in his hand a little firmer. I could barely perceive that the goat was standing motionless on his feet, facing toward the river rather then the mountain. I raised my rifle nearer my cheek and waited. All I could hear were the crickets and the frogs. Then there was a brief sharp noise. I could see the outline of the goat move quickly, and then there was a dull thud of padded feet striking something solid, and then only silence. The goat was still standing.

Rajah Singh cautiously clicked on the flashlight and put the beam on the goat. Then he moved it in the direction the goat was looking. There, twenty-five feet farther away, was the leisurely reclining body of a leopard.

"Shoot! Shoot!" whispered Rajah Singh frantically.

I pulled the trigger, aiming at the left side of the animal's chest, and it sprang out of the beam of light. We jumped out of the blind and rushed the spot. There was blood on the ground and a trail of it ran to the steep, grown-over side of the plateau. We looked over the brink and threw stones down. The cat moved just a few feet down the slope. I couldn't quite see it, and didn't intend to go down after it yet. It had looked plenty big in my sights.

My guide gave a yell at some moving lights far below us and answers came back. Their voices sounded excited and Rajah Singh explained that men were coming to help. While walking back and forth trying to locate the position of the cat, I scrutinized the goat who was still standing, watching us unconcernedly. There was not a scratch on him. Evidently he had dodged the leopard's leap, but because he didn't run the cat knew he couldn't get away and so he decided to take his time about the kill. From then on I called the goat my "pukka" goat -- that means genuine, the real McCoy.

By the time ten men had arrived, we found the cat dead. His spots had blended with the spots of light and shadow made by the flashlight so that we had overlooked him before. He was six feet long, but that included quite a length of tail, and I imagine he weighed about 180 pound. Two men found a pole and tied the feet over it, and then in true safari style, the procession descended the trail.

The G.I.s had been kidding me before we left: "Sa 'ib go 'bang', Sa 'ib bring home goat."

Gabe was half awake when I walked in. He said, "We heard Sa 'ib go 'bang'. Where's the goat?"

I showed him the animal, and then dumped the still-warm cat on him. He jumped out of his blankets and came down standing. The enthusiasm they all showed made the trophy all the more glorious. In the morning the coolies skinned and scraped and cured the hide, and eventually I was able to bring it back to the States with me.

Each of the three tried on different nights to bring in another cat but met with no success, although Hank did see one much larger than mine.

Fishing in the river was poor, so we spent a good deal of time chasing wild pigs up and down mountains with little success. The endurance of the natives was incredible. They could run up a mile of mountain path, while we would walk it in one attempt only by blind painful determination.

In addition to one pig, most of which we gave to the natives, we killed a porcupine, and because our provisions were low decided to make a stew out of one front and one back leg. The meat had a flavor that was entirely new, but we enjoyed it very much.

The six-mile walk back up the mountain was another grueling ordeal in spite of the fact that we had four days of practice. While waiting for the truck to come, we ate lunch on the road just around a curve from town. A few people wandered out to stare at us, and among them was a ragged little girl of the Brahman class, as the ending of her name Jwaladutt indicated. She carried herself with pride that was thrilling to see. She had sharp aquiline features, and she watched closely everything we did. Of all the children she seemed to be the most fearless and so we indicated that we would like her picture. She was perfectly amenable to the idea, and when we paid her two annas her shrewd eyes opened wide. She hastened back to town, and in a few minutes, we had all the children wanting their pictures taken. Among them was Paroli, the beautiful girl whom Gabe was unable to photograph before. Obtaining her picture was a worthy finale to an interesting hunting trip.

The short two weeks ended in hot and filthy trip back to the squadron camp. Other officers were sent off to rest camp and I was needed again to fill in on the flights to Burma. Flying those last two missions was like kissing the Lady Luck a fond farewell. Other men have done it -- plenty of them -- but to me it seemed like living on borrowed time. I was scared.

My total reached thirty-five missions and 320 hours of combat -- I felt that I soon would meet my crew wherever it was they had gone.

Then one evening the Colonel passed me near the mess hall.

"Say, Bill, here's something that will interest you," and he showed me orders promoting me to captain. "And there are more orders down at the office. They say something about sending you home. Three crews are going in a few days."

I felt limp and happy and wanted to cry -- only men aren't supposed to so I didn't. At dinner as I looked at the boys who were staying, I felt guilty. I couldn't blossom out with a big grin and say "Oh Brother! I'm going home!" These boys were as scared as I had been, and they still had hours to put in. I felt like volunteering to stay, but knew darn well I'd be kicking myself numb when this present feeling wore off.

I couldn't see Faith before I left but I sent a telegram and wrote a letter to her which I gave to Allan. She was a grand person and I hated to write her off the books with a cold pen-and-ink goodbye.

In thirty-seven hours after leaving India, we arrived at Accra, where we waited five days for our turn to be flown across the Atlantic. Twenty-four hours later we descended to Miami. I will always remember how my joints ached as I stepped from the cold cramped quarters of the transport in the early darkness, and how my muscles were jittery for the next two weeks. I don't know whether it from excitement at being home or the lack of food and sleep while flying. That same day I reported per orders to the Army Forces Tactical Center at Orlando, Florida and found that I was to help train other men in combat tactics that had been learned the hard way.

Here, perhaps, the narrative should end -- with my basking in the safety and cleanliness of the United States and slowly coming to take the war for granted again in spite of buying war bonds, stamping tin cans flat, saving bundles of paper, and so forth.

But before I had been home three months, fully half of the combat men in my squadron in India had died. The battle for Burma was just underway, and yet people continually said, "Isn't it grand that the war is almost over!" Nine months later we invaded France.

Our men of vision believe the air-routes firmly established around this world-at-war would act like rawhide thongs in the sunshine of post-war life and draw the extremities of the earth together until they are only a few hours and a few dollars apart. The filth and starvation and retarding social chains of some of the world's people could not survive only a few hours from a prosperous and wisely benevolent America. But if these States are not united in understanding the ideals behind the torture, denial, and death of their own fighting men, how can they understand other countries enough to live with them in peace?

The energy of life given up by the thousands of crews who were Ed and Paul and Jerry and Adam and Taylor and the rest, is an energy we can use to maintain peace. I want my children to fly on the airways of the world and see only lighted towns and revolving beacons, not bomb bursts through a pilot's window.

THE END

Printed in the United States
By Bookmasters